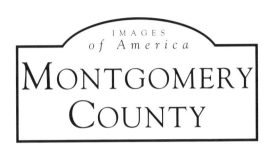

IMAGES
of America

MONTGOMERY
COUNTY

D1599913

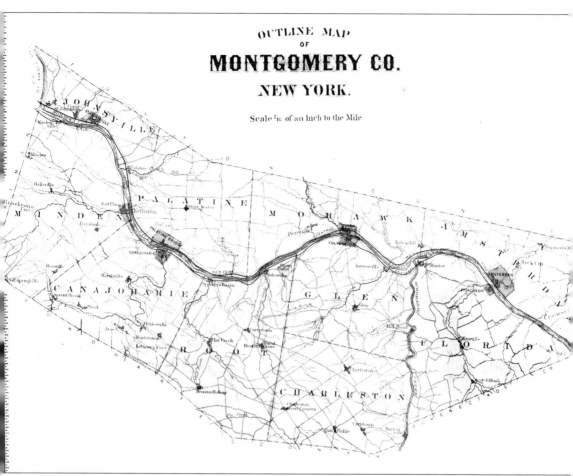

This map of Montgomery County is from the 1868 Stranahan and Nicholas atlas.

IMAGES
of America

MONTGOMERY COUNTY

Kelly Yacobucci Farquhar

Kelly Yacobucci Farquhar

ARCADIA

First published 2004

Published by Arcadia Publishing,
Charleston SC, Chicago IL, Portsmouth NH, San Francisco CA

Printed in Great Britain

Library of Congress Catalog Card Number: 2004108751

For all general information, contact Arcadia Publishing:
Telephone 843-853-2070
Fax 843-853-0044
E-mail sales@arcadiapublishing.com
For customer service and orders:
Toll-free 1-888-313-2665

Visit us on the Internet at www.arcadiapublishing.com

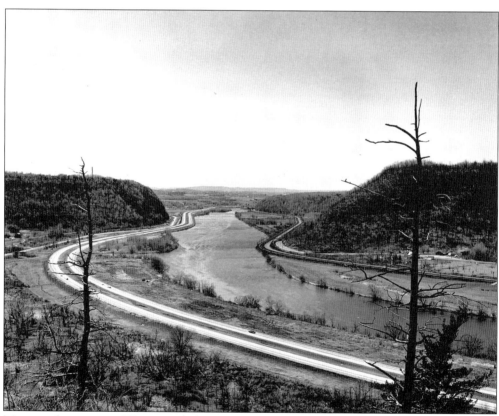

Many settlers moving West passed through Montgomery County's "Noses," as they were the only natural break in the Appalachian Mountain chain from New Hampshire to Georgia.

CONTENTS

ACKNOWLEDGMENTS

As a child, I was always fascinated with discovering the history of the area in which I lived. That fascination has accompanied me into my adulthood. With an ever-changing landscape across our country, sometimes it is difficult to imagine the way our surroundings looked before we were here. The images in this book tell a story of our county and the people who lived here before us. In times when things may look bleak, perhaps seeing what once was will encourage us to attain that level of prosperity again.

Because compiling this book has been such a tremendous project, I would like to thank the following people for their help: my mom, Patricia (Johnson) Evans, for encouraging my love of history for my entire life; my husband, Bryan, for supporting my work, going to my presentations, traipsing through cemeteries with me, and taking care of our baby girl, Mackenzie, so that I could work on the book at home; my staff at the Montgomery County Department of History and Archives for taking on additional workload so I could complete research; the Canajoharie Library and Art Gallery; Sandy Cronkhite, historian in the village of Fort Plain; Lois Gruner of the Charleston Historical Society; Lynda Z. Marino, historian in the town of Root; Anita Smith, historian in the village of St. Johnsville; and Lorraine Whiting, historian in the town of Charleston. They have all been instrumental in supplying me with information and photographs for those areas in which the collection of the Montgomery County Department of History and Archives is lacking.

INTRODUCTION

Located in upstate New York, west of the capital city of Albany, is a little county with big beginnings. Montgomery County, first named Tryon County in 1772 after Colonial governor William Tryon, in its original formation covered a tremendous amount of territory, including a great deal of central, western, and northern New York. The five districts that made up Tryon County were Canajoharie, Palatine, Mohawk, Kingsland, and German Flatts. The massive county extended as far west as the lands of the Six Nations, north to the St. Lawrence River, and south to the Pennsylvania border. At the close of the Revolutionary War, the county was renamed Montgomery in honor of Gen. Richard Montgomery, who heroically died in the Battle of Quebec. From this original entity were created many of the 63 counties that exist in New York State today.

Prior to the settlement of the Europeans, Native Americans inhabited the lands throughout the valley named for the Mohawks, one of the six Iroquois tribes. Early European settlers to this area included the Dutch, in search of trapping and the fur trade, and the Palatine Germans, in search of religious freedom.

The Revolutionary War had significant impact upon the residents of Montgomery County. Four regiments, consisting of enlisted men throughout the valley, made up the Tryon County militia. Blood was shed upon the lands within the county during this time. The battles that took place at Klock's Field and Stone Arabia, not to mention the horrendous incursions by raiders, wreaked havoc. Lives and homes of area residents were ravaged and terrorized by groups who collectively included Native Americans, British troops, and their former neighbors who remained loyal to the Crown.

Travel to the western frontier was more passable through Montgomery County due to "the Noses." Prominent geological features adorning both sides of the Mohawk River, the Noses are the only break in the Appalachian Mountain chain from New Hampshire to Georgia. One significant mode of transportation was the Erie Canal, constructed through Montgomery County. The development of a number of its towns can be attributed to "Clinton's Ditch." In fact, the proximity of the Erie Canal was one of the factors supporting the move of the county seat from Johnstown (now in Fulton County) to Fonda.

Principal farming products in Montgomery County during the Colonial period and immediately after the Revolutionary War centered around grains. Evidence of this type of farming was visible in the construction of the numerous Dutch barns. With the advent of the Erie Canal, however, farming changed from production of grains to dairy farming since the grains could now be transported from farms in the West. With the railroad, agriculture changed once again. As milk was not yet transportable in rail cars, production turned to cheese.

Other industries in Montgomery County have prospered from the waterpower of the various tributaries. Knitting and carpet mills, milk factories, gristmills, glove and sack factories have all gained success from the tributaries of the Mohawk River.

Notable figures such as Susan B. Anthony, Kirk Douglas, and former lieutenant governor of New York Mary Ann Krupsak have left their imprints as either natives or residents of Montgomery County.

In recent years, the county has experienced tremendous change. A once thriving area that fell into decline is now looking toward a resurgence of prosperity. With the immigration of diverse communities, such as the Akwesasne Mohawk Indians, Latinos, and the Amish, and the establishment of their various cultures, Montgomery County hopes to attract a wider tourism audience.

A large portion of the photographs in this book were taken from the collection of the Montgomery County Department of History and Archives. This genealogical and historical research library, with a collection often referred to as one of the largest in the state, welcomes almost 3,000 visitors annually from all over the world in search of their ancestors.

—Kelly Yacobucci Farquhar
Montgomery County Historian and Records Management Officer

One

AMSTERDAM

Originally a part of Caughnawaga, Amsterdam became its own town on March 12, 1793. After the formation of Fulton County in 1838, Perth broke off from Amsterdam, thereby becoming the town's northern boundary. The Mohawk River on the south, the town of Mohawk on the west, and Schenectady County on the east form the other of Amsterdam's boundaries.

The Chuctanunda Creek, flowing through the town and emptying into the Mohawk River, has been the principal influence for Amsterdam's industrial beginnings. Numerous mills cropped up along the Chuctanunda, using the waterpower to assist their operations. In 1860, a reservoir was constructed to provide adequate water supply to the mills, only to be enlarged in 1876 to accommodate the increasing demand.

Montgomery County's only city, Amsterdam was first named Veddersburg after the early settler Albert Vedder and was located near the mouth of the Chuctanunda during the Revolutionary War. By 1804, the name of the settlement had changed to Amsterdam, influenced by the large Dutch population. Incorporated as a village in 1831 and then as a city in 1885, Amsterdam greatly prospered during the late 19th century from the city's carpet, knitting, and broom industries.

Amsterdam's ethnic diversity is clearly evident in the numerous churches and fraternal organizations that formed there. These ethnic groups generally settled in the neighborhoods in which they worshiped.

Port Jackson, on the south side of the Mohawk River in the town of Florida, was annexed in 1888, becoming the city's fifth ward. Hagaman and Fort Johnson, both incorporated as villages in 1892 and 1909, respectively, Cranesville, and Manny's Corners are the other settlements in the town of Amsterdam.

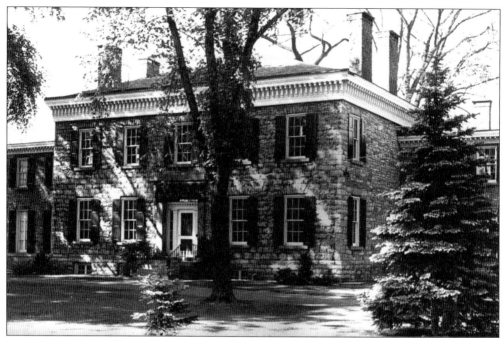

Guy Park Manor, the Colonial home built in 1766 by Sir William Johnson for his daughter Mary and his son-in-law and nephew, Guy Johnson, was confiscated when it appeared the Johnsons would not return from Canadian exile after the Revolutionary War. Following a series of residents, the home was taken over by New York State in 1907 to use while maintaining the Barge Canal. Later used for storage by state engineers, it was rescued by the Daughters of the American Revolution in 1920. Today, its occupants are the Montgomery County Chamber of Commerce and state Assemblyman Paul Tonko.

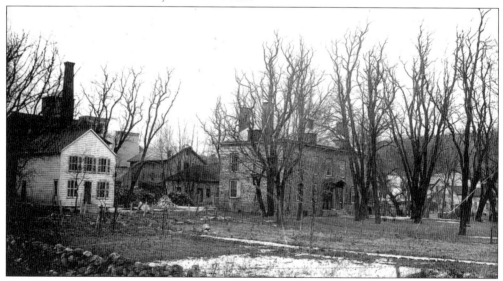

Fort Johnson (center), the 1749 baronial home of Sir William Johnson, served as the headquarters for the superintendent of Indian Affairs and commander of the Mohawk Valley militia during the French and Indian War. After the elder Johnson removed to his new mansion in Johnstown, his son John lived here, along the Kayaderosseras Creek.

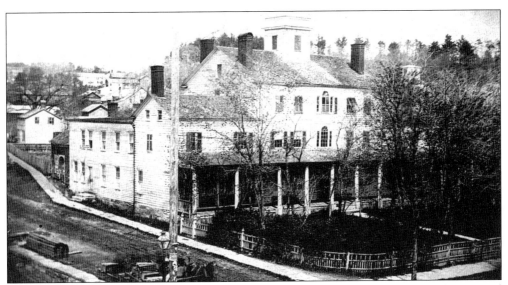

Built at the junction of the Chuctanunda Creek and East Main Street, the Globe Hotel prospered from travel on the Mohawk Turnpike. When business declined after the opening of the Erie Canal, however, it was used for the private education of females. Incorporated by the state legislature in 1839, the Amsterdam Female Seminary, while housing females, provided coeducational instruction during the day. After the school moved to Academy Hill, the building was razed in 1867, and it its place was erected the First National Bank.

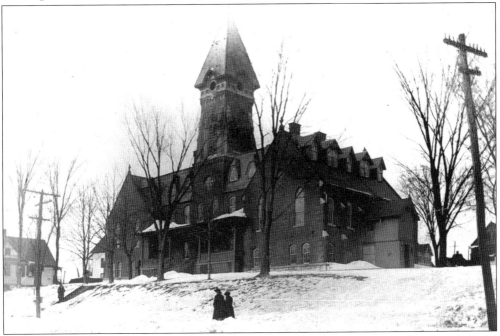

Upon receiving a new charter in 1865, the former Female Seminary relocated to a modernized structure at the top of Wall Street. Sitting atop Academy Hill, the Amsterdam Academy had some of the village's most prominent businessmen on its first board of trustees. By 1895, the schools had combined to form the Amsterdam School District. The growing student population prompted the construction of a larger school on the academy site in 1917.

11

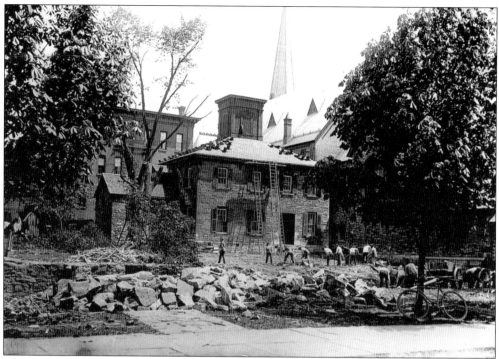

Built in 1838, the Old Stone School was located on Division Street, next to St. Anne's Church. The city's first high school was erected on this site in 1904.

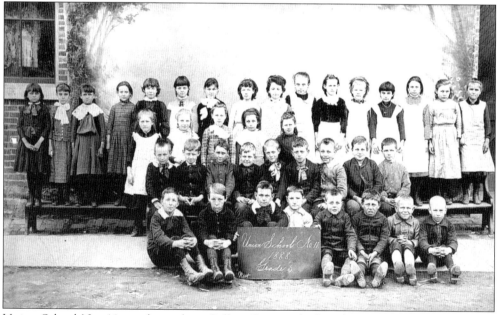

Union School No. 11 was located on Collins Corners (today, the northwest corner of Golf Course Road and Route 30) in the town of Amsterdam. Pictured are students of the school, with the boys in the front and the girls in the back.

Amsterdam City Hospital opened on Division Street in 1889 in response to the industrial city's need for hospitalization. With 18 patients in the first year, medical care for one week, including bed and food, amounted to $5. Nursing personnel came from the school established just west of the hospital. In 1963, when the hospital moved to a 26-acre lot just north of the city limits, the name changed to Amsterdam Memorial.

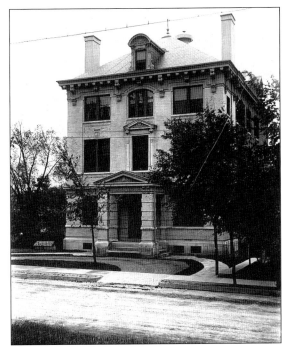

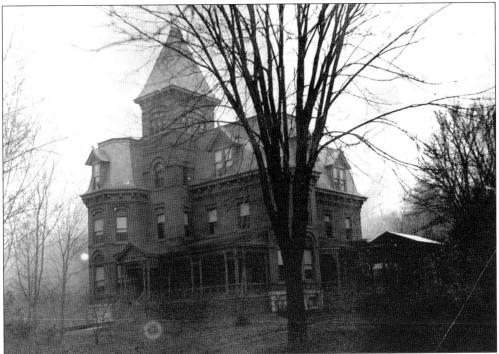

The congregation at St. Mary's Church purchased the home formerly owned by the Marcellus family in 1903. With 27 beds for patient care, the home was opened as St. Mary's Hospital. One enlargement came 10 years later. Due to increasing need for hospitalization, on the 75th anniversary of the opening, the hospital broke ground for further expansion, making room by razing a number of homes along Guy Park Avenue.

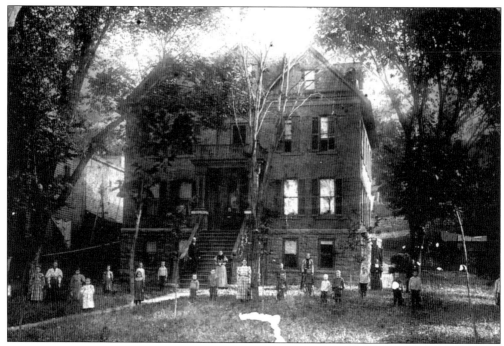

Children's Home Association existed on Guy Park Avenue as early as 1888. In 1896, Stephen Sanford constructed the brick building as a memorial to his son William Sanford. The residence became superfluous when children began being placed in private homes during the 1940s. Some 20 years later, the abandoned building was razed and replaced by the New York State Unemployment Office.

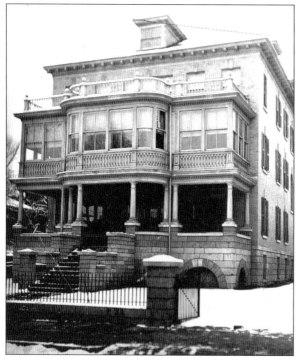

Sanford Home for the Elderly was constructed on Guy Park Avenue in 1906. The home, built by Stephen Sanford in memory of his wife, cared for the city's aging population.

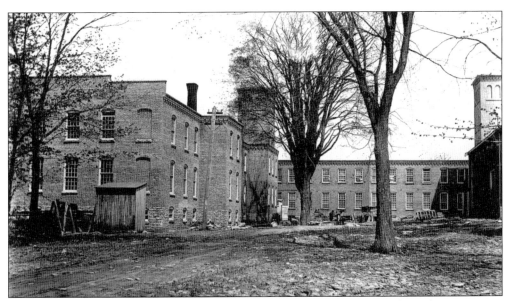

The power supplied by the waters of the Chuctanunda attracted many industrialists to "set up shop" along the banks of the creek. Among those was Henry W. Pawling, who organized and built the Red Star mill in Hagaman, to the north of Amsterdam, in 1881. Red Star employees used trolley transportation to get to work, where they made scarlet and fancy underwear until the mid-1930s. Approximately 15,000 pairs of shirts and drawers were produced here annually. Following various unsuccessful business ventures at the former mill, the building was deemed unsafe and finally was razed in 1991.

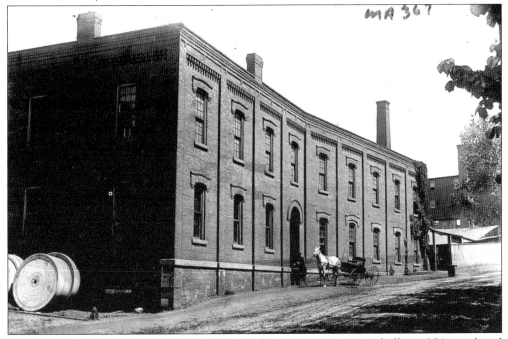

The Shuler Spring Company, located on Church Street opposite city hall in 1856, employed more than 100 workers making carriage springs. By 1869, David W. Shuler's employees had manufactured approximately $200,000 worth of carriage springs.

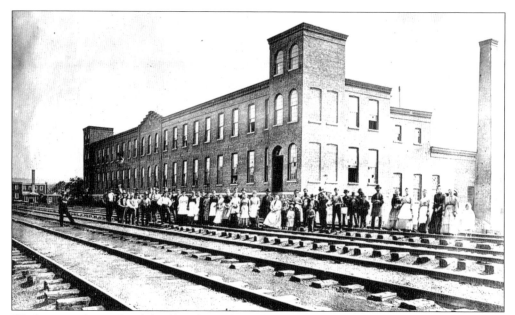

Workers stand outside of the Shuttleworth Brothers Company mill, adjacent to the Mohawk River, in 1884. Beginning operations in 1878, Shuttleworth Brothers was one of the leading carpet manufacturers in Amsterdam. By 1920, the company had consolidated with another major manufacturer, McCleary, Wallin & Crouse, to form the corporation known as Mohawk Carpet Mills.

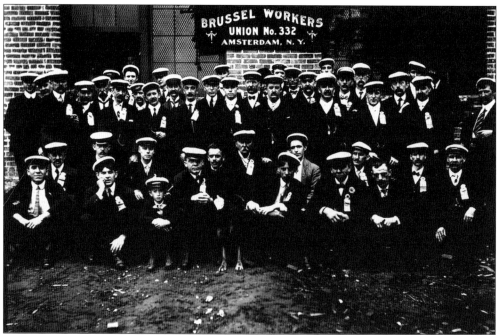

Brussel Workers Union No. 332 at the Shuttleworth Carpet Mills included workers from England. During the first half of the 20th century, Amsterdam became nationally recognized for its carpet-making industries. Shuttleworth became synonymous with longevity in the carpet industry, spanning 100 years.

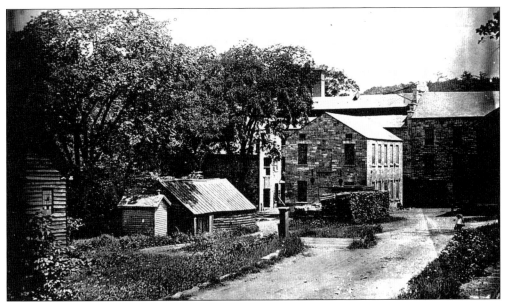

The Kellogg & Miller factory started in West Galway in 1824. Moving operations to Amsterdam in 1851, the factory had produced up to 6,000 gallons of linseed oil by 1900. Linseed oil, created by pressing seeds from the flax plant, is primarily used in paint thinners and industrial cleaners.

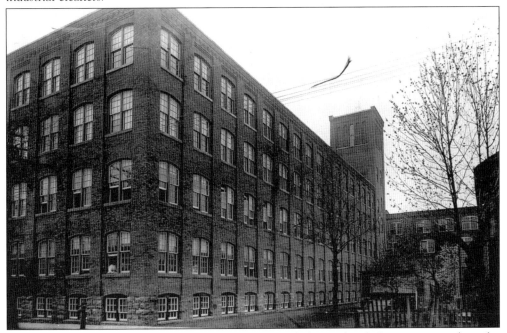

Broomcorn, locally grown on the islands and flats of the Mohawk River, was used in the production of brooms. The Blood family established the Pioneer Broom Company, one of the area's largest broom manufacturers, on Washington Street in 1902. The company then moved to the six-story building constructed on West Main and Pine Streets two years later. Production continued until the 1930s, when use of brooms fell into decline with the invention of the vacuum cleaner.

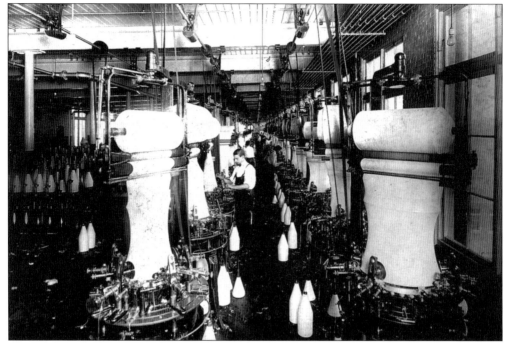

Although known as "the Carpet City," Amsterdam was about as prolific in the knitting industry as in that of rug making. The Chalmers knitting mill was one of the last major knitting mills to be organized in the city, in 1901. Located on the south side of the Mohawk River, Chalmers manufactured the well-known Porosknit, which received national attention through a huge electric sign over Times Square in New York City.

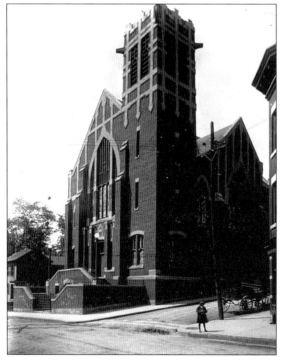

The Zion German Lutheran Church split from the Trinity Lutheran congregation before 1890 and moved back to the framed building originally occupied by the Trinity Lutherans on Grove Street. The Zion Lutherans, in 1909, built a brick church at the corner of Grove and Liberty Streets. This church was taken down when the western section of Route 5 was made arterial, essentially removing Grove Street.

St. John the Baptist Catholic Church was built in 1912 to provide a house of worship for the increasing Polish population, believed to be one-third of the city's total populace at one time.

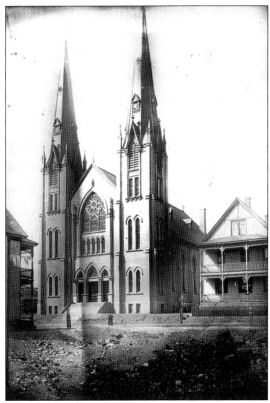

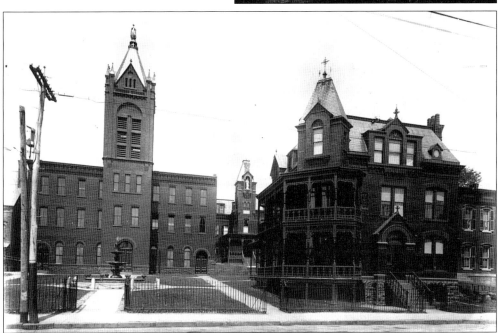

St. Mary's Institute, chartered by the New York State Board of Regents in 1881, was the county's first parochial school. The parish complex, on East Main Street, included the institute, the convent housing the sisters of St. Joseph of Carondelet, and the rectory.

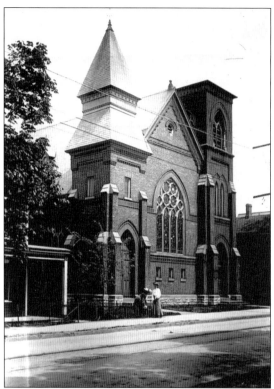

The city's predominately German population in the mid-to-late 19th century led to the establishment of numerous congregations for that ethnic community. The German Methodist Episcopal Church was constructed on Division Street, between Wall and Pine Streets, in 1886.

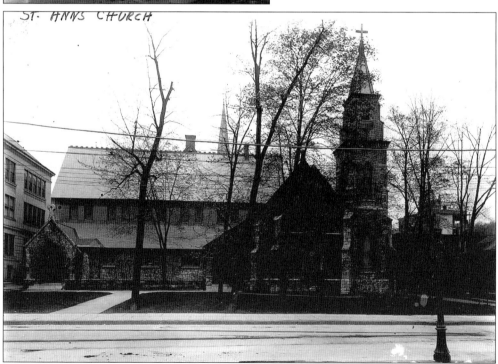

Descending from Queen Anne's Chapel in Fort Hunter, St. Anne's Episcopal Church congregation worshiped in Port Jackson prior to constructing this church on Division Street.

St. Stanislaus's Church, located on Cornell Street, was the first of Amsterdam's churches to attend to the religious beliefs of the Polish immigrants. The church was built in 1896, and a school was established 10 years later for the elementary education of the congregation's children.

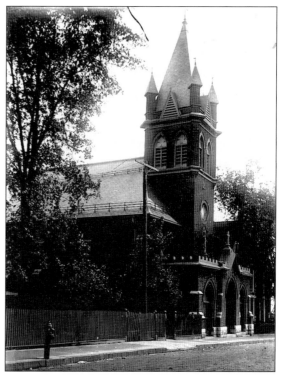

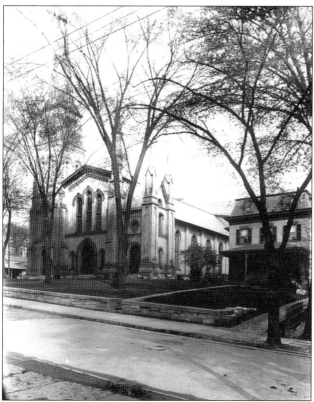

The Second Presbyterian Church, on the corner of Church and Grove Streets, was the second building to occupy this space. The first structure was razed in 1869. The second edifice was built of brick in 1870. The sanctuary contained a number of Tiffany stained-glass windows. Sadly, the church and its windows were destroyed by fire in January 2000, and a third church has since been constructed.

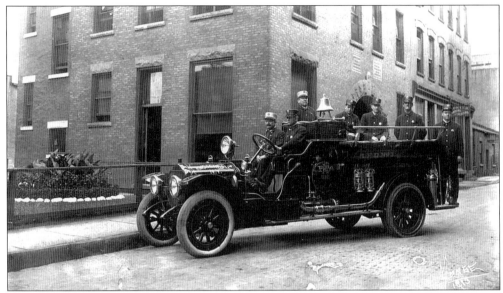

Sitting on the fire department's first motorized truck, from left to right, are Chief Stichel, David Hare, assistant James Brady, Edward Mackringer, Peter Riley, Michael J. Donohue, and James J. Stewart. The truck was purchased in 1913. The Mohawk Engine Company, established in 1839 as Amsterdam's first fire department, was one of seven volunteer companies phased out by 1907 and replaced by paid companies.

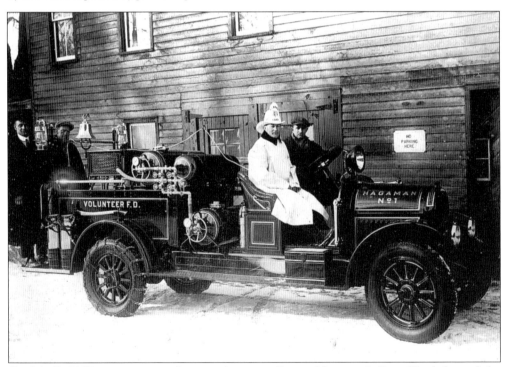

On July 7, 1925, meeting attendants at the post office in Hagaman's Briar Block formed the Hagaman Fire Department. The first firehouse, on William Street, was purchased from Lewis Harrower in 1938 for $400. It was used until the present site was purchased in 1950.

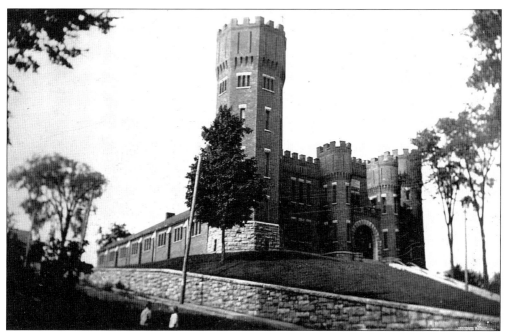

Resulting from an 1894 mandate by New York State, Montgomery County constructed a facility on Florida Avenue for the local National Guard. The $45,000 armory provided the 46th Separate Company—later redesignated Company H, 2nd Battalion, 2nd Regiment—with space for holding drills, which became essential in 1898, during the Spanish-American War.

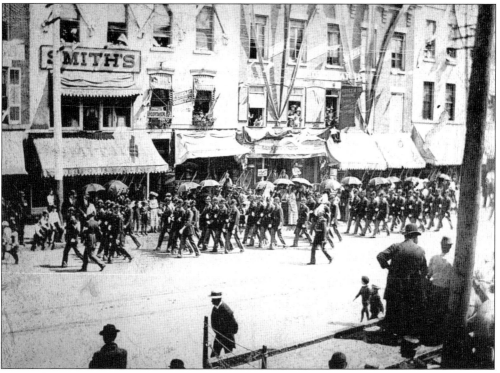

The 46th Separate Company marches in Amsterdam on August 15, 1891.

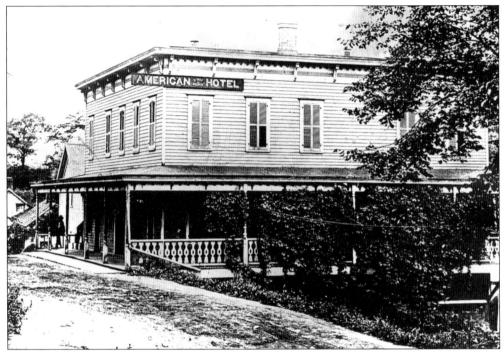

Haverly J. Way's American Hotel in Hagaman entertained village dignitaries making the first trolley trip between Hagaman and Amsterdam on July 30, 1902. The trolley ran parallel to the Chuctanunda Creek. This photograph shows the hotel approximately three years after that trip.

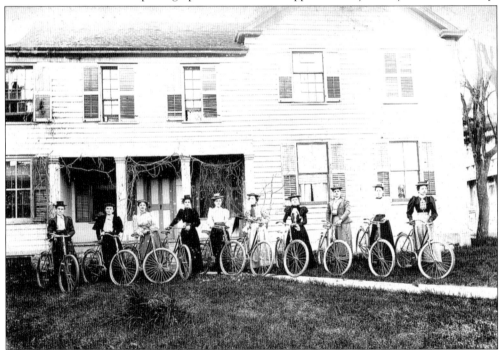

The women of the Hagaman Bicycle Club pose in front of a home on Haskell Street c. 1907. Maude Blanch Mosher stands second from the left.

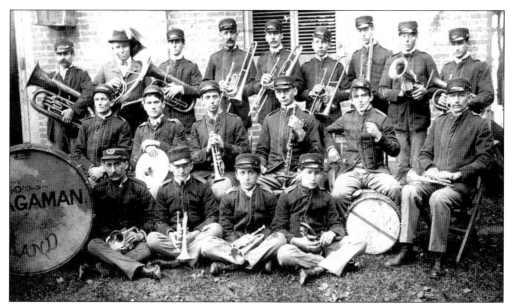

The 1901 Hagaman Band included the following, from left to right: (first row) F. Bowan, Herbert Breen, M. Fowler, and M. Fowler; (second row) E. Davis, J. Lang, G. Wilkens, C. Cook, C. Hillman, and F. Hayden; (third row) B. Barity, E. Wood, R. Irving, A. Snyder, G. Person, F. Ming, M. Shook, G. Luck, and F. Davis.

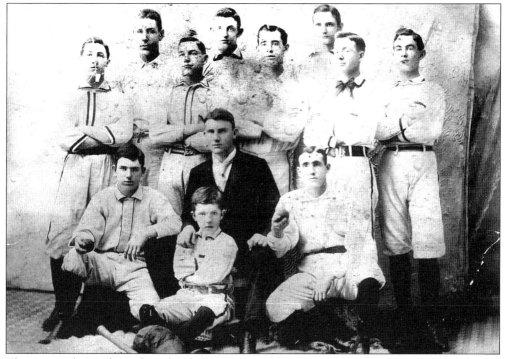

The Amsterdam Independents baseball team poses in 1895. Pictured here, from left to right, are the following: (first row) Jack Shananan, catcher; Thomas Bradley, manager; Dick Nolan, pitcher; and Jim Riley, mascot; (second row) Michael "Mickey" Donohu, Ben McKinney, Mike ?, Joe Morgan, Peter Collins, Thomas Madden, ? Burns, and Jack ?.

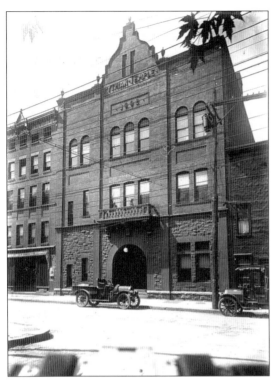

With a membership of approximately 500, the Knights of Pythias erected its meeting place, the Pythian Temple on Spring Street (Guy Park Avenue) below William Street, in 1892. The structure was the first of those constructed by the city's fraternal groups.

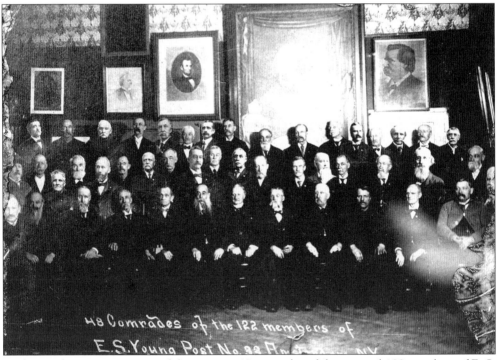

Gathering for an anniversary celebration are 48 comrades of the original 122 members of E. S. Young Post No. 33 of the Grand Army of the Republic (GAR). The veterans group organized on April 10, 1875, and met at the GAR hall, above 45 East Main Street.

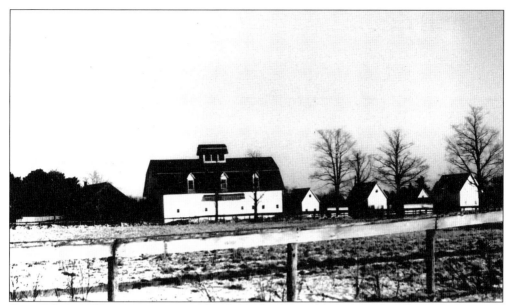

Consolidating about 1,000 acres of local farmland, Stephen Sanford established Hurricana Farm in the late 1870s. Housing thoroughbreds that raced at Saratoga, Hurricana also had a half-mile outdoor track, an indoor track, and lavish outbuildings that were once home to the 1916 Kentucky Derby winner. The third generation Sanford at the farm, Stephen "Laddie," became the first American to win the English Grand National in 1923.

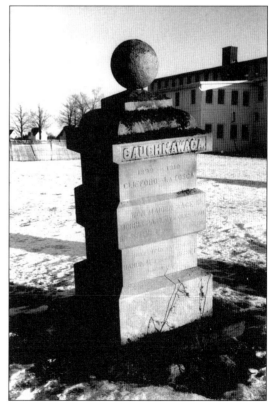

The racehorse Caughnawaga is buried at Sanford's Hurricana Farm in the town of Amsterdam. Markers such as this were erected for the horses that had won turf honors at the farm. Although many of the buildings have been razed in the development of shopping centers, some of these markers can still be seen from Route 30 North.

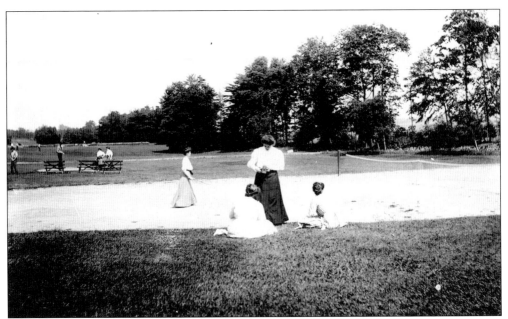

Frank M. Blaisdell, a Boston architect also credited with creating the Sacandaga Park, designed the 18-hole golf course at the Antlers Country Club. While their husbands took to the course, "golfing widows" enjoyed the beautiful Mohawk Valley vista from the clubhouse veranda or took to a game of tennis.

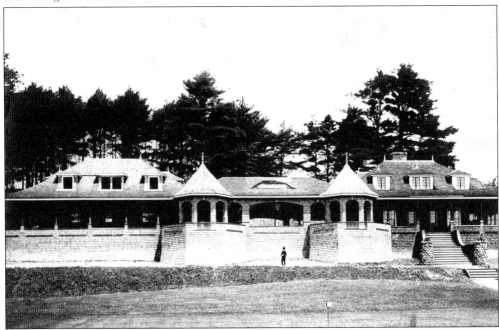

Prosperity in Amsterdam in the latter 19th and early 20th centuries allowed time for leisurely activities. The Antlers Country Club, organized in 1900 by wealthy businessmen, was designed as a place for the social elite. Due to the numerous social engagements that attracted the who's who of Amsterdam, the clubhouse was enlarged in 1904. Destroyed by fire in 1965, it was replaced by a smaller version, minus the spacious veranda.

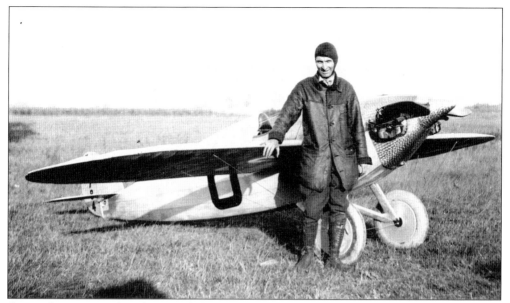

Amsterdam native Edward B. Heath (1888–1931) test-flies one of his Baby Bullet racing planes on August 19, 1928. Having tested his first aeroplane at the Antlers Country Club in 1910, Heath went on to sell planes in kit form. His Chicago-based company also became a major supplier of hardware to firms constructing planes used during World War I. Heath died when testing his Low Wing model in 1931.

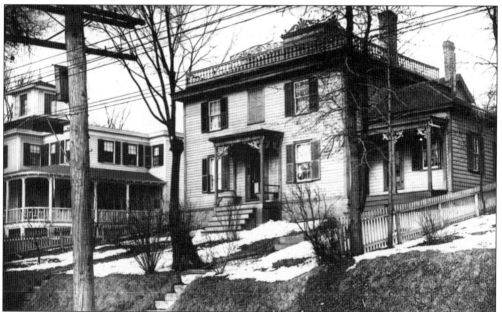

The pictorial history of Amsterdam's industrial era was thankfully preserved by one man, musician John A. Maney (1870–1935). A native of Troy, Pennsylvania, Maney settled in Amsterdam and, through his hobby of photography, collected images of the architecture, various industries, and historic sites since lost in the name of progress. These images were thankfully saved from destruction when a neighbor rescued them from the curb following Maney's death.

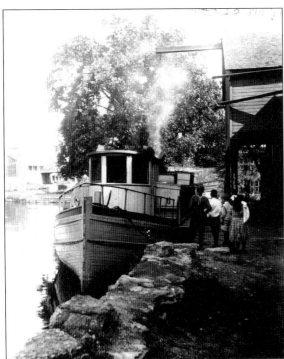

This Erie Canal boat makes a stop at Port Jackson. Businesses in small communities along the Erie Canal started and thrived with the packet boats transporting freight and passengers. It was not uncommon to see children traveling with parents who owned canal boats.

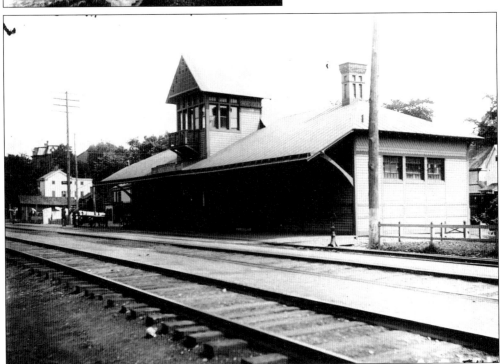

In order to compete with the New York Central Railroad north of the Mohawk, the West Shore Railroad began operating a station at Port Jackson on the south side in 1883. The passenger and freight stations here were renamed South Amsterdam when Port Jackson was annexed to the city in 1888.

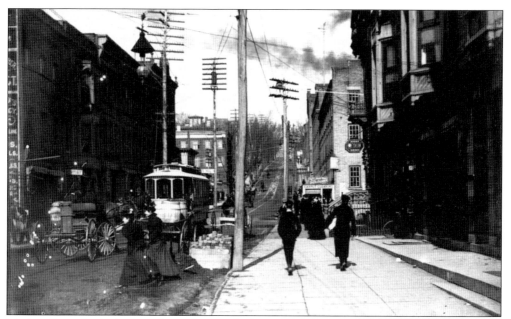

Market Street looked relatively modern in the late 19th century, with trolleys, telephone lines, and electricity. In 1881, the Amsterdam Telegraph and Telephone Company operated a switchboard of 50 lines. Trolleys first made their way up Market Hill in 1891, and by 1897, Market Street was illuminated with electrical streetlights.

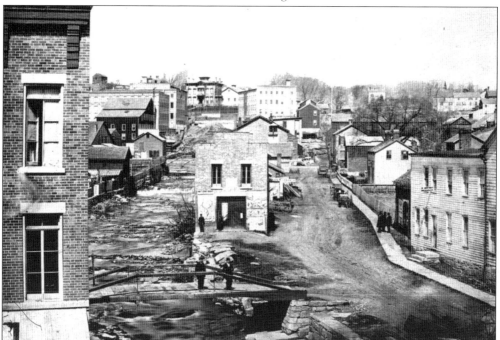

Chuctanunda Creek and Street are seen in the late 19th century. Between them is an old fire station that became a police station. Note the street lamp and telephone pole in the lower right corner. At this time, the streets were not yet paved and carriages were still the primary mode of transportation.

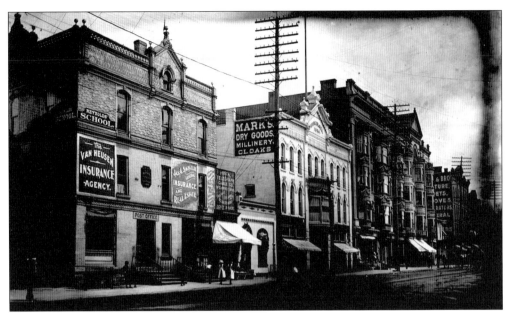

The corner of Church and East Main Streets may have looked this way during Kirk Douglas's formative years in Amsterdam. Born in the city to Russian immigrant parents, Issur Danielovitch, later known as Kirk Douglas, graduated from Wilbur H. Lynch High School in 1934 before achieving fame as an actor in Hollywood.

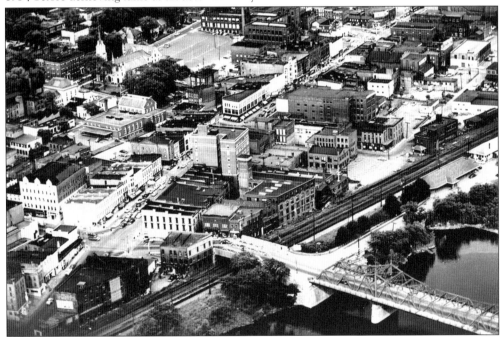

This aerial view of downtown Amsterdam captures the heart of the city's business district prior to urban renewal. Almost 400 buildings, remnants of the city's industrial zenith, were demolished in the later 1960s and early 1970s to allow for replacement structures and parking lots. Arterials cut through the downtown business section. Many reminisce about the stores and thoroughfares lost to progress.

Two
CANAJOHARIE

With the formation of Tryon County in 1772, one of the five original districts comprising the county was Canajoharie, taking its name from the creek so designated by the inhabiting Mohawks. The district's boundaries stretched much farther than those of the present township. Located on the south side of the Mohawk River, the district extended from the Noses west to Fall Hill, outside of Little Falls. The town of Minden was formed on the western front in 1798. Today, the town continues to be bordered on the north by the Mohawk River and extends southward to the Otsego County line.

Primarily settled by German Palatine immigrants, the lands in the town were fertile for farming. Numerous homesteads were fortified in Canajoharie during the Revolutionary War.

The attraction of the waterpower drew settlers to locate near the creek, operating mills from the mid-1700s. Although early settlement was sparse, the population gradually increased, and on April 30, 1829, the area closest to the river became incorporated as the village of Canajoharie.

Ames, in the southern portion of the township near the Schoharie County line, was the smallest incorporated village in New York State in 1924. Other hamlets in the town of Canajoharie include Buel, Marshville, Sprout Brook (the birthplace of industrialist Henry J. Kaiser), and Mapletown.

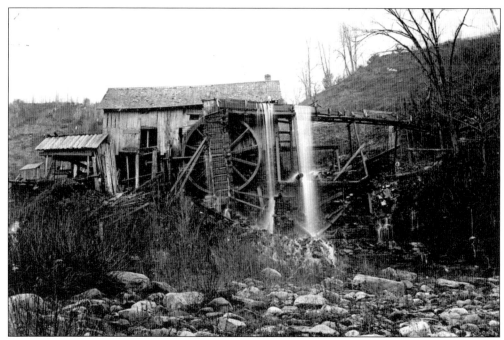

This old mill used waterpower from the Canajoharie Creek starting *c*. 1770. Once belonging to an early settler, the mill was in a state of decline when nearby Arkell & Smith began operations there almost a century later.

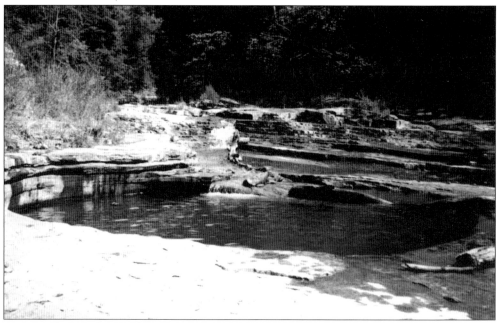

Can-a-jor-ha, or "the pot that washes itself" to Native Americans, is a cavity in the bed of water that flows through the town. The cavity is 20 feet in diameter and more than 10 feet in depth. The swirling rocks and water supposedly caused the cisternlike shape. Early settlers adopted this name for the area in which they had settled. Although a natural beauty, the Canajoharie gorge has proven deadly, and visitors are prohibited from swimming in the creek.

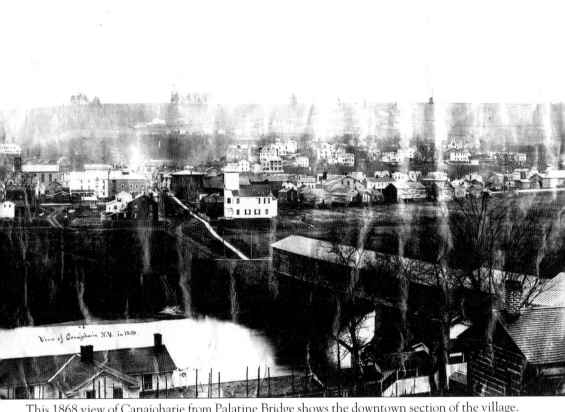

View of Canajoharie N.Y. in 1868.

This 1868 view of Canajoharie from Palatine Bridge shows the downtown section of the village. The white-framed church building was first constructed in 1818 as a union church for all denominations in the small community. Previous to its location here, the structure had been located beside the Erie Canal's towpath, which ran alongside its exterior wall. Because of the canals's proximity, music from the packet boats often disrupted services.

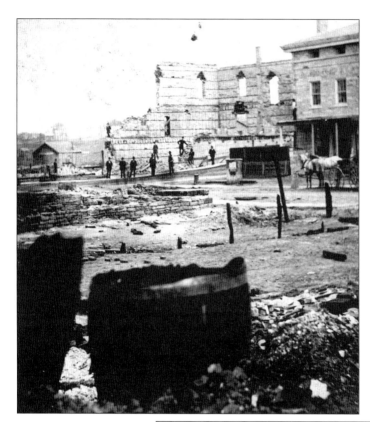

The fire of April 30, 1877, the third great conflagration in the village's history, caused extensive damage to the business district. More than $250,000 in property damage was recorded. The two previous fires had ravaged virtually the same area, from the canal south to Main Street, in 1840 and 1849.

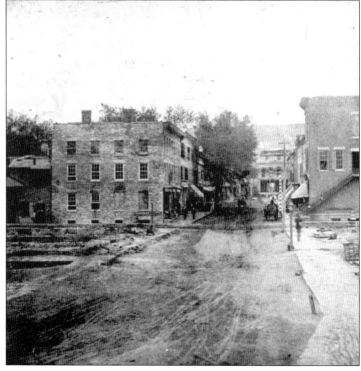

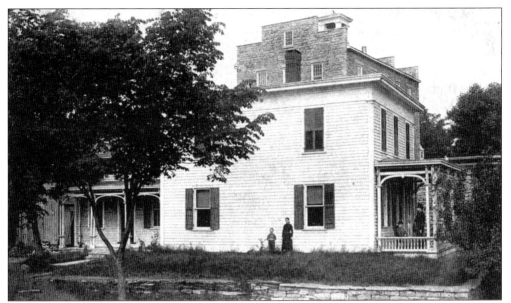

The Barrett home stood on the corner of Rock and Cliff Streets. Pictured here are, from left to right, Charlie Barrett, Bell Barrett (born c. 1874), and Cornelia and William Barrett (village constable). The former academy building presides over Canajoharie's west hill, behind the Barrett home.

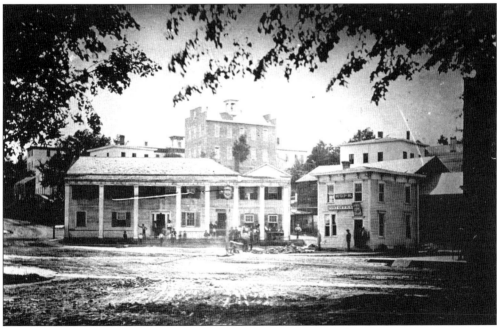

Downtown Canajoharie looked quite different c. 1876–1878. The Eldredge House Tavern, constructed in front of Schrembling's (later Roof's) stone tavern, was razed in 1878. The Hotel Wagner was then built on this site. The stone structure at the top of the hill is the Canajoharie Academy, occupying the site prior to the former West Hill School. To its right is the first academy building, the wood-framed school where Susan B. Anthony served as preceptress before joining the women's suffrage movement.

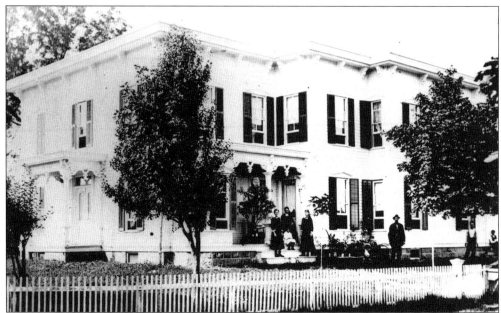

Pictured at the Bowman home, on South Buel Road, in 1883 are Bertha Bowman Bellman, Effie Bowman Kinaman, Cora Bowman Van Deusen, Charlotte Jones Bowman, Elisha Livingston Bowman, and some hired hands. The Central Asylum School for the Deaf and Dumb instructed students in sign language and practical living. One of four such schools in the country at that time, Central Asylum operated in Buel from 1823 to 1836. Robert Bowman, father of three deaf children, donated the land for the school, possibly nearby this future home.

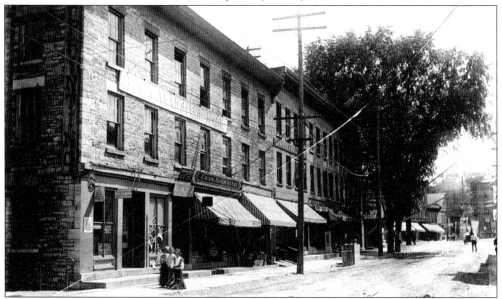

The *Canajoharie Radii* office stands at the southeast corner of Church and Main Streets. Levi Backus, a former teaching assistant at Buel's School for the Deaf, first published the newspaper in 1837. Below the *Radii*'s masthead, Backus printed the newspaper's name in the written form of the manual alphabet. He was the first publisher to receive appropriations from New York State for the circulation of his newspaper to deaf-mute residents.

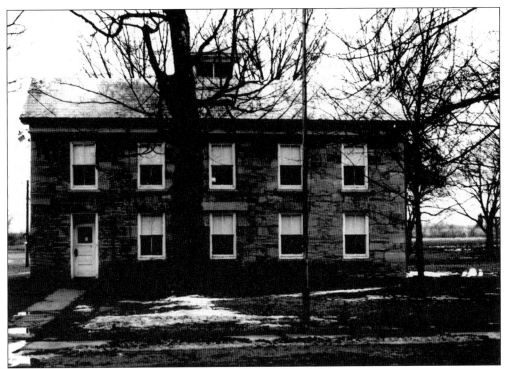

Among those students schooled at the Ames Academy was Ames native Alexander Randall (1819–1872). Randall went on to achieve success as the postmaster general of the United States and was twice elected governor of Wisconsin (1857 and 1859). The hamlet of Randall, in the town of Root, was named in honor of this Montgomery County native son.

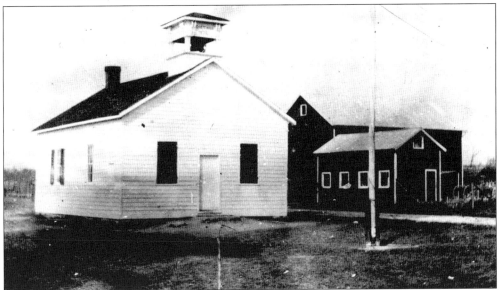

The Old Marshville School appears here c. 1910. Built on land donated by Seymour Marsh, for whom the hamlet of Marshville was named, the schoolhouse was constructed through local residents' donations of money, lumber, and time. The centralization of the Canajoharie School District in the early 1950s left the schoolhouse vacant.

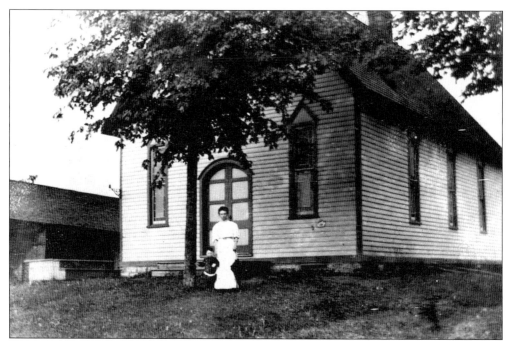

Marshville residents needed not only a schoolhouse but also a place to worship. Religious services were held in the schoolhouse until funds could be raised to erect the Marshville Evangelical Church in 1892.

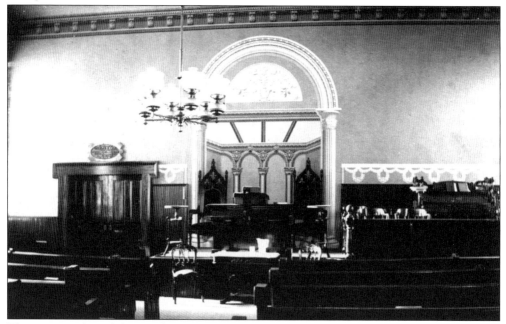

The interior plan of the Mapletown Reformed Church, constructed in 1852, was not unique. With the congregation facing the entrances, the small rural church did not accommodate the anonymity of members tardy to the afternoon services. Although the church itself was razed in the early 1970s, an association oversees the continued maintenance and burials in the adjoining cemetery.

After worshiping in the union church for several years, the congregation of the Canajoharie Reformed Church organized in 1827 under the leadership of Rev. Douw Van O'Linda. John Frey donated the Front Street land on which the church was erected in 1842.

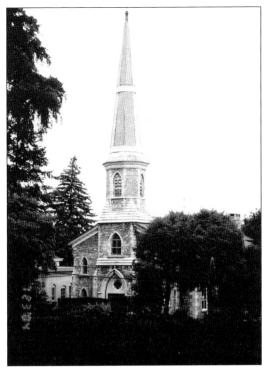

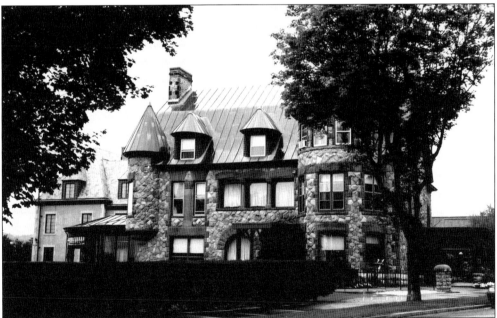

Arkell Hall, the magnificent home of Sen. James Arkell and his family, has graced Canajoharie's east hill since 1891. The palatial grounds, landscaped with small pools, rare trees, and flowering shrubs, elegantly adorned the original home, constructed more than 30 years earlier. Arkell's daughter, Bertelle, lived on the estate with her husband, Frank Barbour, until death, and in her will, she made provisions to open the house to elderly women between 1951 and 1952.

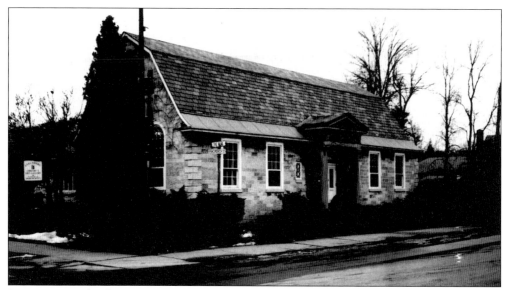

Beginning in the home of Minnie C. Arkell, wife of William J., in the early 1900s, the Canajoharie Library and Art Gallery was not formally recognized by the board of regents until 1914. Built at its present location, at the corner of Church Street and Erie Boulevard, in 1925 by Bartlett Arkell, the library has undergone a series of renovations to accommodate its growing collection. Home to a vast collection of Beech-Nut artifacts and works from 19th- and 20th-century artists, the gallery also houses a large Winslow Homer collection and a full-size replica of Rembrandt's *Night Watch*.

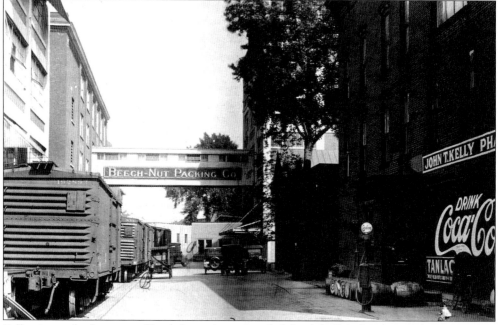

Following in the footsteps of his father, who cofounded the Arkell & Smith sack factory, Barlett Arkell became the first president of the newly formed Beech-Nut Packing Company, then named the Imperial Packing Company, in 1891. Local farmers would sell their produce to Beech-Nut for use in the widely known baby food.

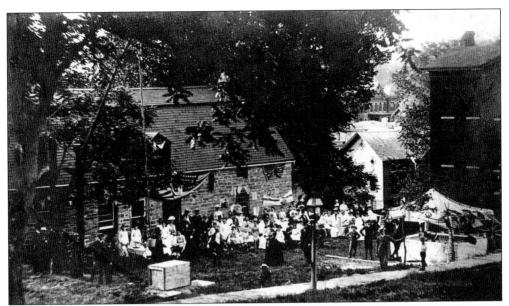

Many enjoy the festivities at the Van Alstyne homestead on July 4, 1888, after the building had undergone repairs and restoration. Built in 1750 by Marten Janse Van Alstyne, the homestead was the site of many meetings of the Tryon County Committee of Safety in 1775.

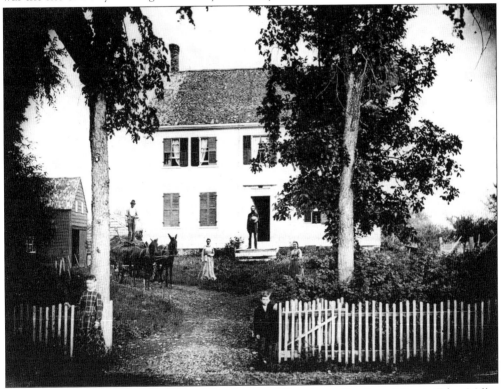

Pictured here in 1876 at the A. B. Miller farm on West Ames Road are Minnie Edna Miller Hilts, John Adam Miller, Peter Armstrong (the hired hand), Josephine Eliza Miller Bellman, and Abram Benjamin Miller (on the porch) and his wife, Anna Eliza C. Bowman Miller.

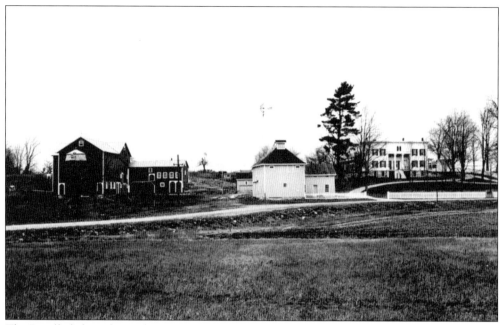

The Retallick farm, located off Route 10 in Marshville, raised hops. The building in the center is a traditional square hop house with a cupola. The kiln for drying the hops was below the cupola. The photograph was taken *c.* 1895.

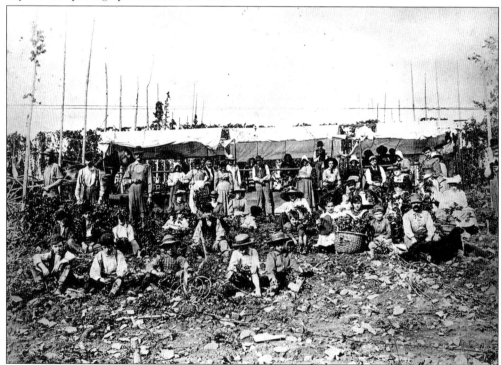

Workers, possibly at the Retallick farm in Marshville, take a break from hop picking *c.* 1895. More than 531,000 pounds of hops were harvested in Montgomery County in 1864. This was a significant cash crop in the towns south of the Mohawk River,

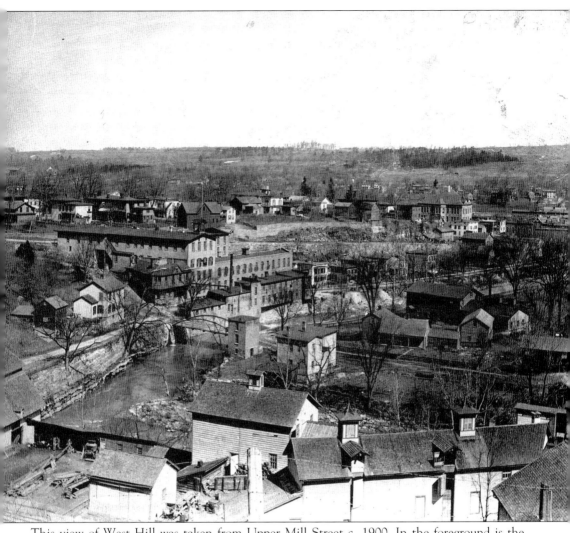

This view of West Hill was taken from Upper Mill Street *c.* 1900. In the foreground is the Bierbauer brewery, and along the west side of the Canajoharie Creek are the buildings of the Arkell & Smith sack factory, which manufactured the first paper sacks. The West Hill School, designed by famous architect Archimedes Russell, was constructed in 1892 using locally quarried limestone.

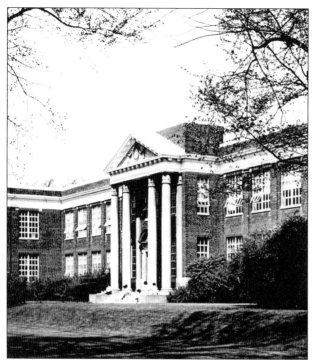

William Lyon & Son of Herkimer was awarded the contract to construct the high school on Erie Boulevard. The contractors broke ground for the foundation on October 3, 1927. After seeing about 70 graduating classes stroll through its halls, the building was razed in November 2002. (Courtesy of the Canajoharie Library & Art Gallery.)

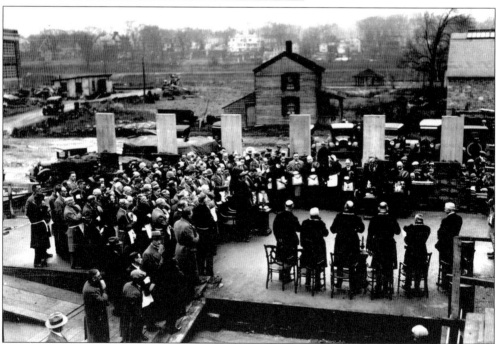

Approximately 200 masons from across the Mohawk Valley and between 400 and 500 area residents attend the ceremony for laying the cornerstone of Hamilton Lodge No. 79 for the Free and Accepted Masons. The ceremony was held on Saturday, December 1, 1928. Laid in the cornerstone were items such as 1928 coins of various denominations, recent copies of local newspapers, and lists of past masters and present officers and members.

Three

CHARLESTON

Formed as a township on March 12, 1793, Charleston was previously a part of Tryon County's Mohawk District. Much of the land in Charleston was included in the 1737 Corry Patent. Named for Charles Van Epps, the nephew of early settler Philip Van Epps, Charleston was reduced to half its original size with the formation of the townships of Glen and Root in 1823.

Located in the southeast portion of Montgomery County and bounded by Schenectady and Schoharie Counties, Charleston is the only township in Montgomery County not bordering the Mohawk River. The rural township contains many small settlements: Burtonville, the site of the earliest development, previously called Mudge Hollow; Eaton's Corners; Cumming's Hollow, settled in 1820; Rider's Corners; Oak Ridge; and Charleston Four Corners.

Population declined significantly in the second half of the 19th century, dropping by 1,000 residents from 1840 to 1890. A principal cause for this decline were the antirent wars occurring between local farmers and landowner George Clarke. Clarke had raised the annual rents that his ancestor, from whom he inherited the land, had granted for a term of three generations. As a result, irate farmers, refusing to pay the increase, set aflame their crops and buildings and left the area. Fortunately, reforestation in the township occurred during the 20th century, providing almost 7,000 acres of renewed vegetation.

Little is known about Charleston's early history, as records were lost in an 1867 fire in Oak Ridge.

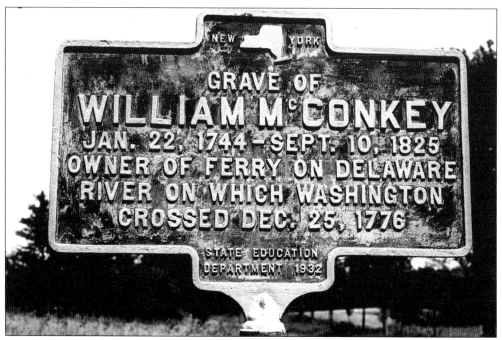

Travelers through Montgomery County get a sense the area's rich history from the historical markers placed near the roadsides. William McConkey (1744–1825), an Irish immigrant, settled in Charleston after helping out during the Revolutionary War. On Christmas night in 1776, McConkey ferried Gen. George Washington and his troops across the icy Delaware River to make their successful early morning attack on the Hessians in Trenton, New Jersey.

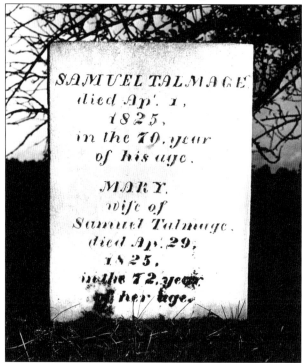

Long Island native Samuel Talmage (1755–1825), as adjutant of the 4th Continental Regiment, New York Line, participated during the Revolutionary War in the Battle of Saratoga, the Clinton-Sullivan expedition against the Iroquois Six Nations, and Lord Cornwallis's defeat and surrender at Yorktown. Talmage and his family transplanted to Charleston, where he is buried, along with William McConkey, in the Second Dutch Reformed Church cemetery, about one-quarter mile west of Rider's Corners on Route 30A.

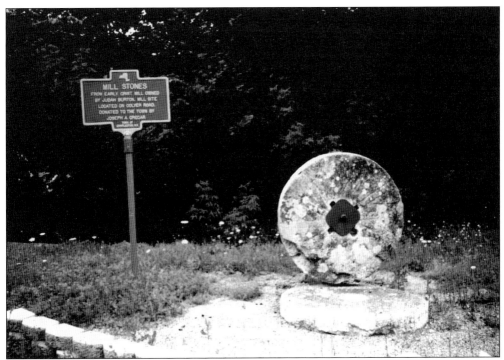

The first gristmill in Charleston was built in 1785 by Judah Burton, who was granted a one-mile square tract of land that later became known as Burtonville. About one mile from the present hamlet, Burton's mill was the only one in town for many years, operating until 1814. These millstones, now displayed across from the Burtonville Firehouse, were removed from the former Burton's mill site, on Colyer Road.

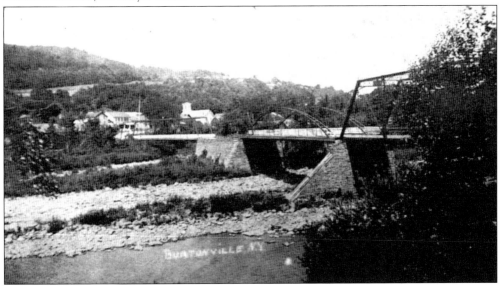

Likely the earliest settlement in Charleston, Burtonville is a hamlet in the southeast corner of town, across the Schoharie Creek from the Schenectady County line. Area settlers were required to maintain the first bridge across the creek, built in 1790. Since then, three more bridges have been erected, the most recent replacement in 1998 by the state.

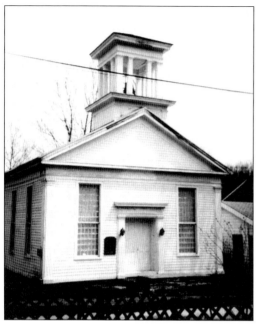

Organized in 1857, the Methodist Episcopal church was one of two churches located in the hamlet of Burtonville. The Christian Church, organized in 1865, was the other. (Courtesy of Lorraine Whiting, Charleston historian.)

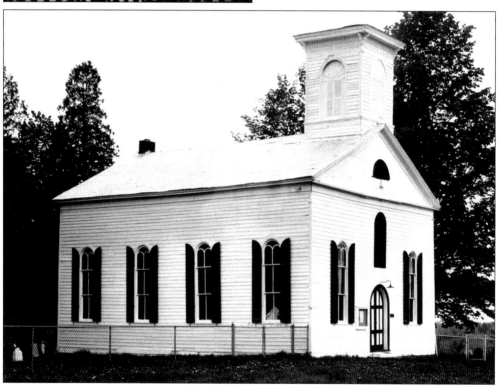

The First Baptist Church congregation of Charleston, at Ryder's Corners, organized in 1793. Rev. Elijah Herrick served as pastor for some 50 years. After burning and being reconstructed, this church edifice fell into disrepair from lack of use and vandalism. Fortunately, it was saved from further damage in 1978 by a group of concerned residents who purchased the Polin Road building and began its restoration. It is now the home of the Charleston Historical Society.

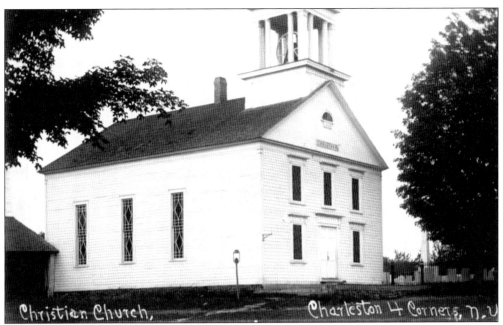

Christian Church, Charleston 4 Corners, N.Y.

In December 1813, a congregation known as the Church of Christ organized in Charleston. First assembling in the 1819 union church building, the members soon erected their own structure at the present location on East Lykers Road at the Four Corners. By 1834, having outgrown the confines of its walls, the old church had been replaced by the present building.

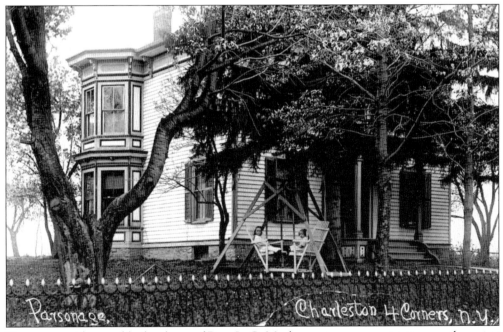

Parsonage, Charleston 4 Corners, N.Y.

Two young girls, possibly daughters of Rev. L. C. Mackay, enjoy some quiet time on the swing in front of the Christian Church parsonage at Charleston Four Corners *c.* 1916. (Courtesy of the Charleston Historical Society.)

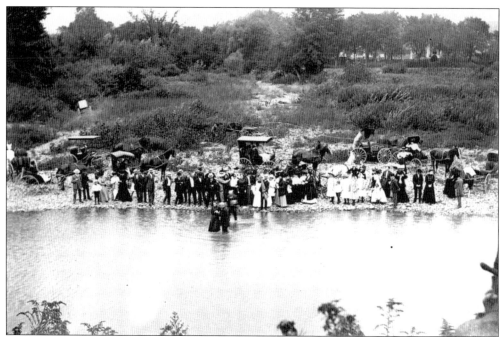

Friends and relatives watch from the shores of the Schoharie Creek near Sloansville as members of the Christian Church at Charleston Four Corners are baptized on September 18, 1910. The Reverend Adelbert Welch was pastor at that time. Almost a century earlier, a group of Free Will Baptists had organized the congregation. The Christian churches of Rural Grove, Burtonville, Randall, and Carlisle were all branches of this church. (Courtesy of the Charleston Historical Society.)

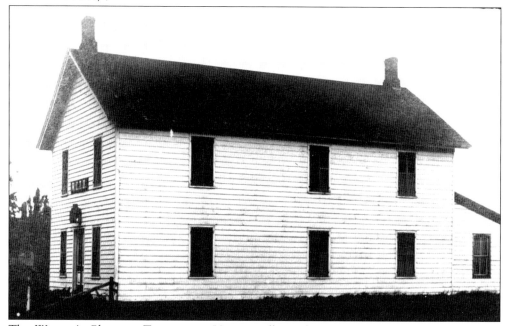

The Women's Christian Temperance Union Hall was located at Charleston Four Corners. (Courtesy of Lorraine Whiting, Charleston historian.)

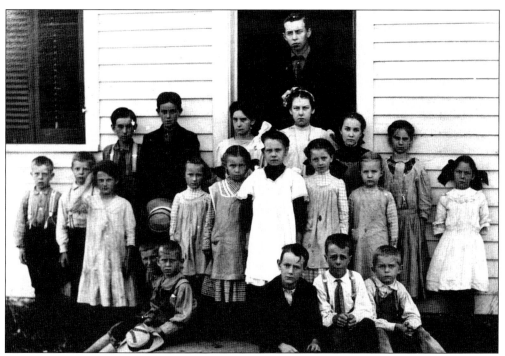

Students and their teacher stand in front of School No. 4 at Oak Ridge *c.* 1910. (Courtesy of Lorraine Whiting, Charleston historian.)

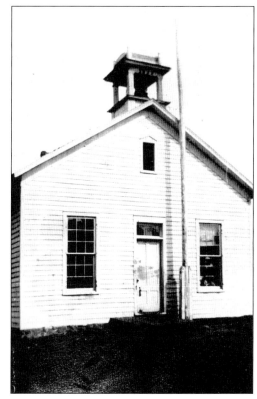

School No. 2, on Corbin Hill Road, was School No. 11 before the restructuring of the town's school districts. (Courtesy of Lorraine Whiting, Charleston historian.)

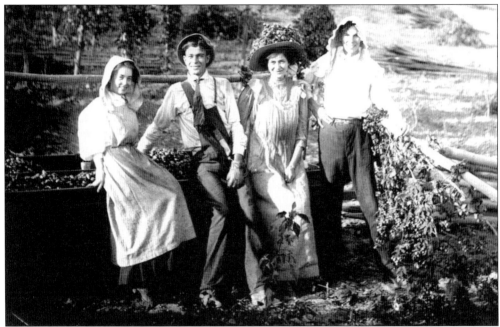

By 1864, approximately two and one-half tons (5,600 pounds) of hops had been harvested in the town of Charleston. From left to right are Myra Montanye, Vernon and Stella Campbell, and an unidentified guest. Note the hops used as trimming for Stella Campbell's hat. (Courtesy of the Charleston Historical Society.)

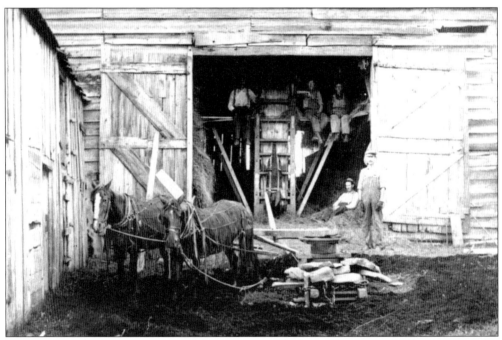

Men work with horses by a barn that was possibly located in Burtonville. Note in the background the windlass and jump-press for haying. (Courtesy of Lorraine Whiting, Charleston historian.)

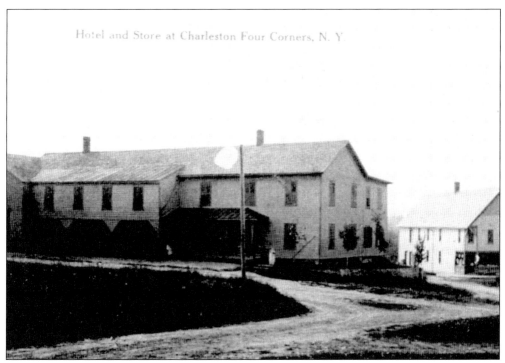

The hotel at Charleston Four Corners was located on the northwest side of Route 162. Conover's (later Kitchen's) Store is visible in the right background. (Courtesy of Lorraine Whiting, Charleston historian.)

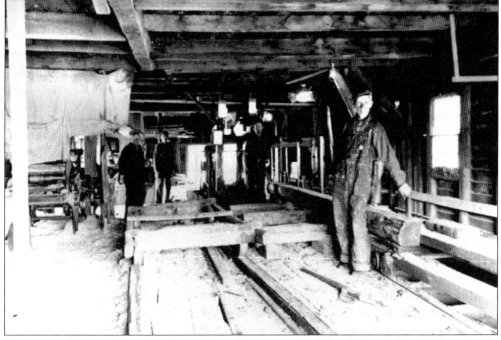

Upstairs in the sawmill at Charleston Four Corners are Fred Frank, Lee Allen, Hudson Frank, and Charles Mallett. (Courtesy of Lorraine Whiting, Charleston historian.)

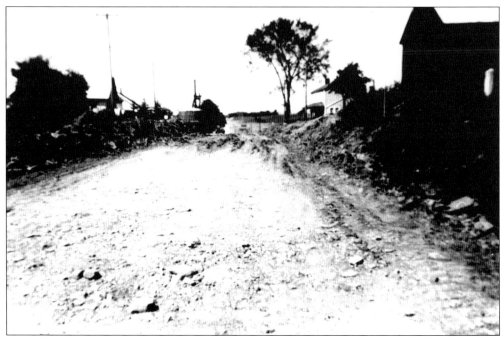

The Sloansville–Rural Grove Highway, also known as state Route 162, saw many improvements in 1931, 1951, and again from 1967 to 1969. Shown is one of the renovation projects, in which some hills were removed and the dirt transported to the other end of town. Directly behind the telephone pole on the left is the old town building. (Courtesy of Lorraine Whiting, Charleston historian.)

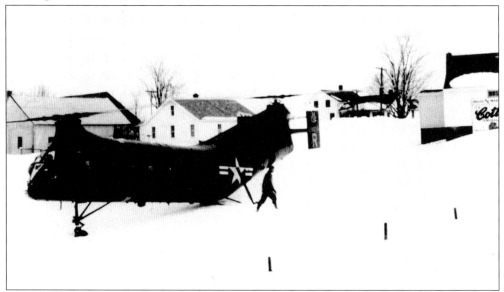

In February 1958, tremendous snowfall blocked transportation. Food and supplies for Charleston residents and their animals were airlifted in by the U.S. Army. Here, an army helicopter lands on Lykers Street, with the intersection of Route 162 to the rear of the chopper. The Basil Davis house is on the left, and the Frank house is in the background. (Courtesy of Lorraine Whiting, Charleston historian.)

Four

FLORIDA

Formed as a township on March 12, 1793, Florida is bordered on the north by the Mohawk River, east by Schenectady County, south by Schoharie County, and west by Glen.

European settlement began in Florida in 1705 with the John Peterson Mabie Patent. In 1712, Queen Anne ordered construction of a palisaded military outpost to defend and protect the Mohawk Indians and settlers from French attacks. The outpost, named Fort Hunter after New York's governor, included a garrison of about 20 men. No longer needed, the fort was razed sometime after the Revolution.

In 1738, Sir William Johnson arrived in the Mohawk Valley to maintain his uncle's 14,000-acre Warrensbush tract in Florida. He was a success in the valley as a trader and, eventually, as Britain's strongest ally of the Iroquois.

In this area rich with agricultural industry, wheat was the township's principal crop.

A stagecoach line from Albany to Canajoharie ran through Florida. Hamlets in the town are Minaville (named in honor of Mexican-American War hero Gen. Francis Mina), Fort Hunter, Mill Point, and Scotch Bush.

Today, the town's renewed prosperity is largely anticipated, with commercial ventures, such as Target Distribution Center, in the industrial park.

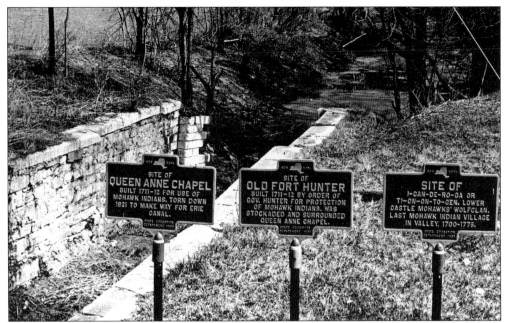

Three markers near the Schoharie Crossing Visitors Center represent various periods in Montgomery County history: "the lower castle," a Mohawk settlement on the Schoharie Creek; Fort Hunter and Queen Anne's Chapel, both built in 1711 at the instruction of England's queen to protect and "Christianize" the natives; and the bed of the Erie Canal. After the Revolutionary War, the vacant fort was taken down and the chapel was removed to make way for the Erie Canal.

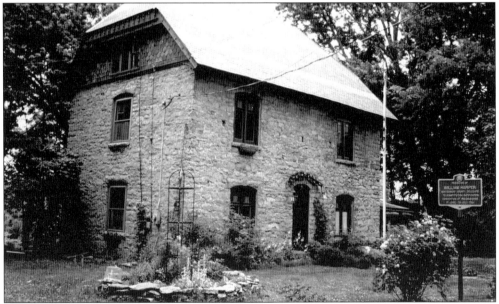

Queen Anne's Parsonage, in Fort Hunter, was constructed in 1712, making it the oldest structure in the Mohawk Valley west of Schenectady. Now a private residence, the parsonage once housed the missionaries sent to the area during Queen Anne's efforts to convert the Native Americans to Christianity.

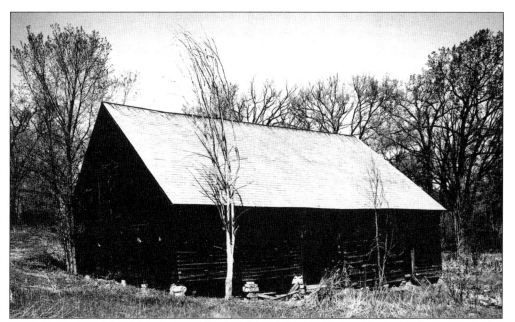

Jan Wemp's Dutch barn was reportedly the oldest barn in the county. Wemp, an early settler to the area, was granted a patent in 1737. A traditional Dutch barn, used primarily for housing grain and perhaps a few family cows, it had an east–west orientation and a center aisle. A large Dutch door opened on each gabled end. This barn, like so many, was removed and reconstructed in another county.

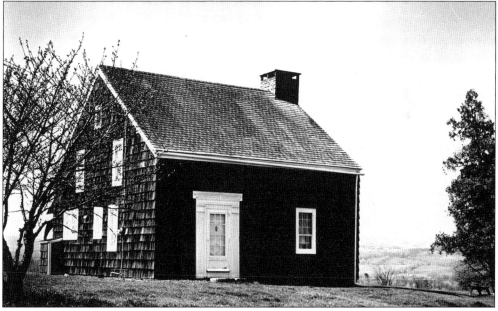

This private residence, located on Simser Road, once belonged to the family of Samuel Pettengill. A captain in Fisher's regiment of the Tryon County Militia, Pettengill left a widow and 13 children when he died at the Battle of Oriskany. During Butler's raid in 1781, Pettengill's widow and family fled the farm to escape the approaching enemy. The family returned unharmed to find everything destroyed.

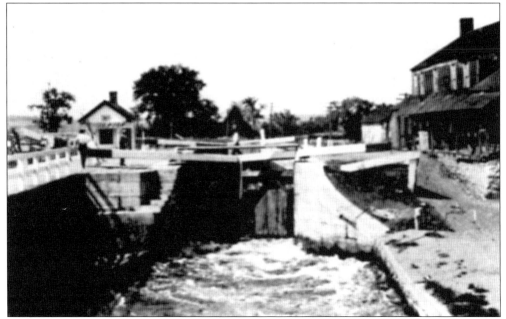

Significant for its proximity to the Schoharie Aqueduct, Lock No. 30 was a part of the enlargement of the Erie Canal in 1841. Brown's Lock Store, at Fort Hunter, provided general supplies for travelers. Now filled in, the lock had once had a lift of 10.5 feet.

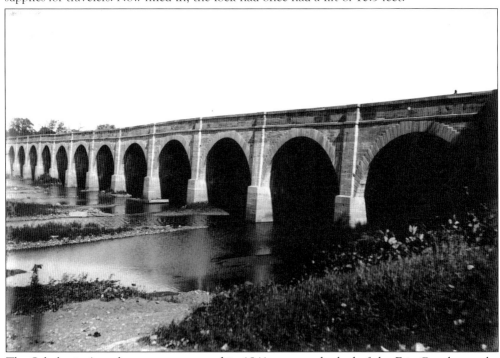

The Schoharie Aqueduct was constructed in 1841 to carry the bed of the Erie Canal over the Schoharie Creek. The previous system of the guard lock and tow team had proved inadequate in overcoming the dangerous flood conditions that arose each spring and fall when the canal flowed through the creek. Sadly, these same conditions have contributed to the aqueduct's slow demise.

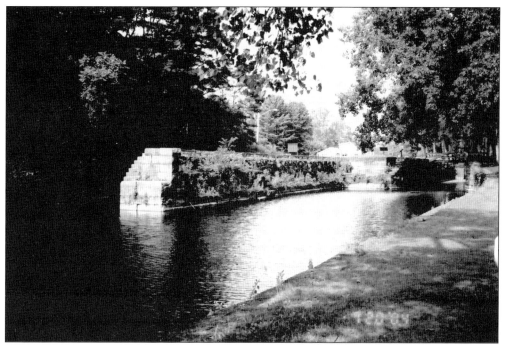

Yankee Hill Lock No. 28, at Fort Hunter, was the last double lock on the improved Erie Canal to be completed in New York State. Well preserved, the historic landmark is now maintained by Schoharie Crossing State Historic Site.

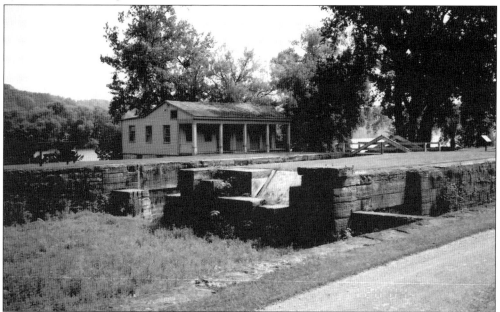

Putman's Lock Grocery, also at Fort Hunter, was owned by the Garret Putman family from 1855 to the 1900s. Canalers could shop for provisions on the main floor and get refreshments at the tavern in the basement. Living quarters for the family and lodging accommodations were available for rent. The store closed in 1917. In the 1930s, the building was damaged, but not completely destroyed, by a fire.

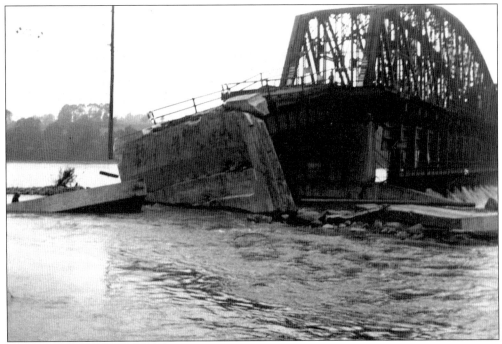

Heavy rains and swollen waters at the confluence of the Schoharie Creek and the Mohawk River have been a consistent problem for the bridge spanning the Mohawk between Fort Hunter and Tribes Hill, as evidenced by this fall 1939 collapse. The bridge has been closed a number of times in recent years due to the same problem.

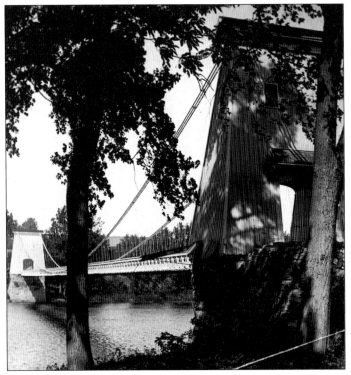

Built in 1852 by the Roebling Bridge Company of New Jersey (builders of the Brooklyn Bridge), this span operated as a toll bridge between Fort Hunter and Tribes Hill for many years. The bridge tender lived at the tollhouse on the Fort Hunter side. Suspension cables were made of one-eighth-inch straight wire bound together. On a windy day, the bridge would swing up to four feet. Free access was provided after local towns purchased ownership from the stock company in 1910. By 1926, New York State had condemned the bridge; it was removed nine years later.

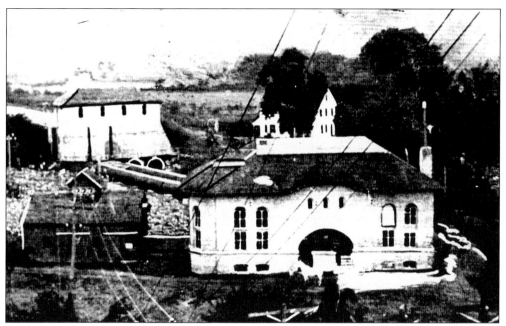

The 1880s saw the age of electricity arrive in Montgomery County. In 1899, the Empire State Power Company began using waterpower from the Schoharie Creek at Mill Point to generate electricity. Above is the powerhouse for the station at Mill Point. Water was diverted to the powerhouse by a 12-foot-high dam through a stone and brick gatehouse. Below are the pits in the basement for the turbines. Steel pipes carried water to the turbines. The venture lasted only 12 years.

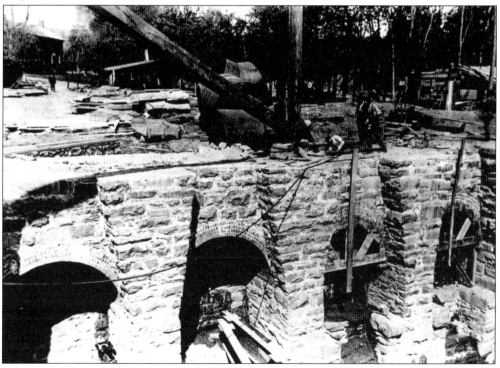

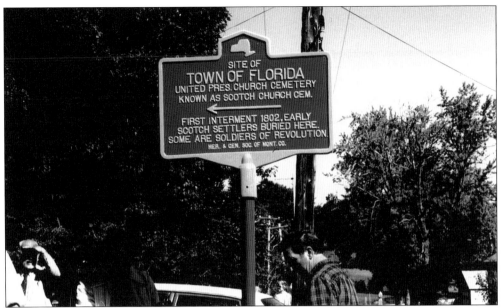

The United Presbyterian Church, commonly referred to as "the Scotch Church," was located near the Schenectady County border. The community consisted primarily of Scottish settlers who had come to the area at the end of the Revolutionary War. Two churches were constructed on the site, in 1800 and in 1846. Today, a historical marker and the cemetery that once adjoined the church mark the location. The first burial in the cemetery occurred in 1802.

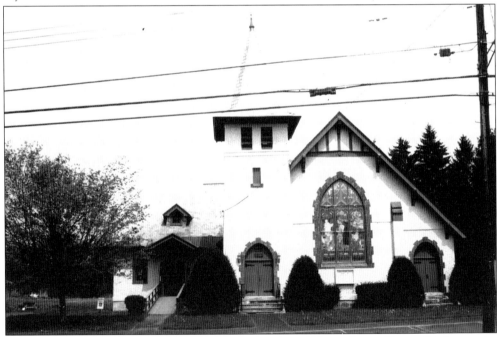

The Florida Reformed Church is located in the hamlet of Minaville, on Route 30. Across the street is the Smith-Cady-Brown residence, now Brown's House Bed & Breakfast. Elias Brown, who served as a brigadier general in the Civil War, and his wife, Louisa, once owned the house and store. (Courtesy of Tim Sievers, Florida historian.)

Five

GLEN

Acquiring its name from early settler Jacob Sanders Glen, the town of Glen was formed from the town of Charleston on April 10, 1823. Bordered on the east by Florida, the south by Charleston, the west by Root, and the north by the Mohawk River, Glen has relatively little flat land. The Auries Creek flows through the town.

An early patent was granted to John Scott, an officer garrisoned at Fort Hunter, in 1722. The tract contained 1,500 acres of land between the Auries Creek and present-day Fultonville. Dutch immigrants, the Quackenbosses settled in this area and established a trading post at which Native Americans were the principal patrons. In 1750, John Evart Van Epps obtained 900 acres of marshland that became known as Van Epps's Swamp. The moniker was later changed to Fultonville, honoring steamboat inventor Robert Fulton.

With a store opened by John Starin in 1810, Fultonville's early development accommodated canal builders and workmen. Streets and commercial enterprises, such as a distillery, potashery, blacksmith shop, and flour and paper mills, were operating by the time the Erie Canal opened. The canal's enlargement attracted additional businesses to Fultonville's hub. The village incorporated in 1848.

A native of Fultonville, John H. Starin became a shipping magnate and, from his prosperity, bestowed numerous gifts upon his hometown.

The hamlet of Glen, first known as Voorheesville, was also an important center of business due to the considerable traffic through the five corners.

Auriesville, east of Fultonville, also flourished with the Erie Canal. This small hamlet had two hotels, a blacksmith shop, a school, and a church, and in much earlier times, it was the site of the Mohawk Indian castle Ossernenon.

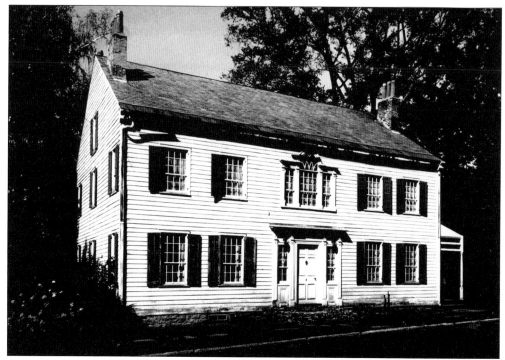

Peter Voorhees built the Edward Edwards house in the historic hamlet of Glen *c.* 1795–1796. The Georgian-style residence, which once served as a tavern, has retained its original staircase, moldings, and mantels crafted by Elijah Pi, a chief of the Stockbridge Indians.

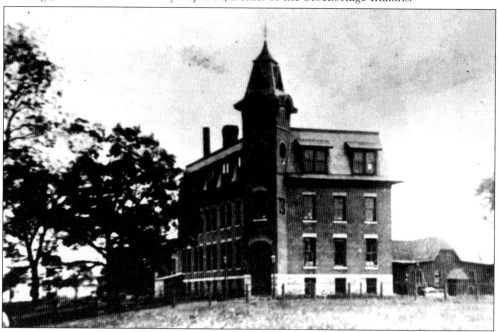

Later known as the Mohawk Glove Corporation, the Starin silk mill became one of the nation's leading producers of silk products (underwear, gloves, hosiery) in the early 20th century. The Buckhorn Truck Stop now occupies the site of the former mill.

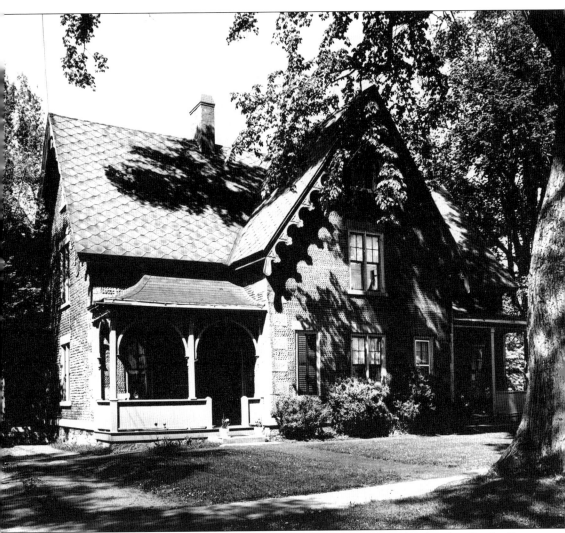

Located on Broad Street in Fultonville, Cobblestone Hall was built by local author Jeptha R. Simms in 1840. During construction of the three-story, 12,000-square-foot home, children were reported to have received up to 25¢ per day for finding stones of the correct size to use in the structure. Later purchased by John H. Starin and used as a sewing school, "the Hall" also had a village library and housed workers from the Starin Silk Mill.

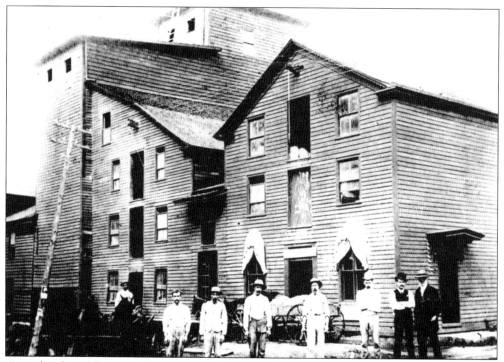

As with other villages in Montgomery County, Fultonville prospered from travel on the Erie Canal. Peter Van Antwerp & Son ran a mill and grain elevator on the south bank of the canal, adjacent to the Donaldson Block. The site is now covered by a New York State Thruway overpass bridge.

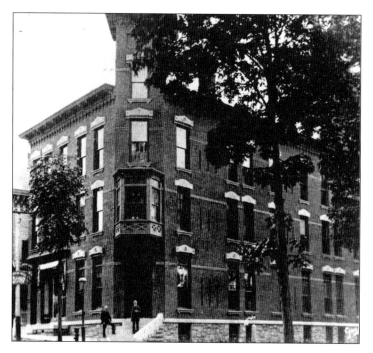

Built in 1883 at the corner of Main and Broad Streets with funds from John H. Starin, the Fultonville National Bank was not exclusively the scene of financial transactions.

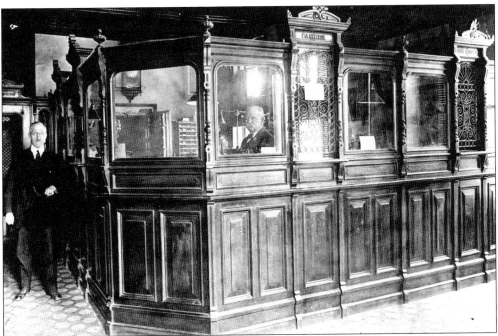

President of the Fultonville National Bank, Alfred DeGraff (left) is pictured with cashier O. F. Conable *c.* the 1890s. Behind the counter is the vault, which became the only remnant from the August 1, 1920, fire that destroyed the bank. The present bank building was constructed around the undamaged vault, which was continually used at the end of the 20th century.

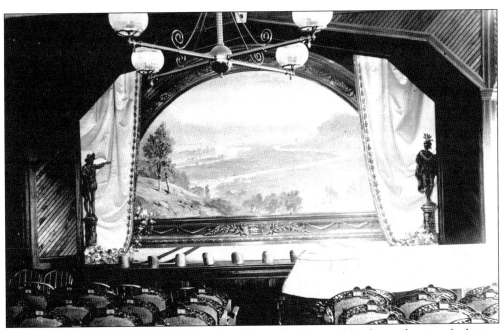

With a hall and stage on its upper floor, the Fultonville National Bank was the site of religious gatherings, high school graduations and balls, and meetings of the Masons and Eastern Star.

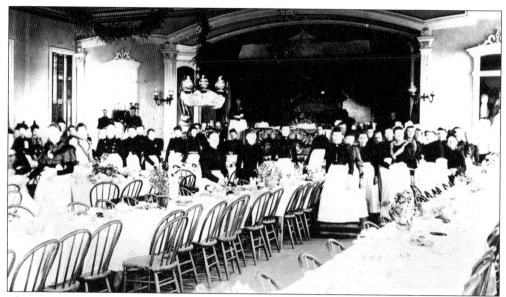

The Montgomery County Sunday School Convention was held at the Donaldson Block hall on November 14, 1893. More than 1,000 meals were served. The Reformed church had three long tables, and the Methodist Episcopal and Baptist churches each had one table.

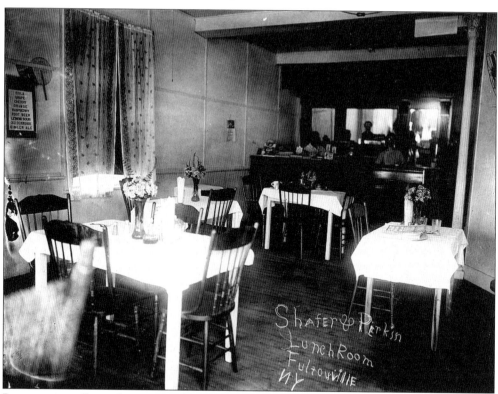

Patrons can still see the counter from the old Shafer & Perkin Lunch Room in the former Donaldson Block. Although the decorations are a little different, the old-time atmosphere remains the same at Sundae's Past.

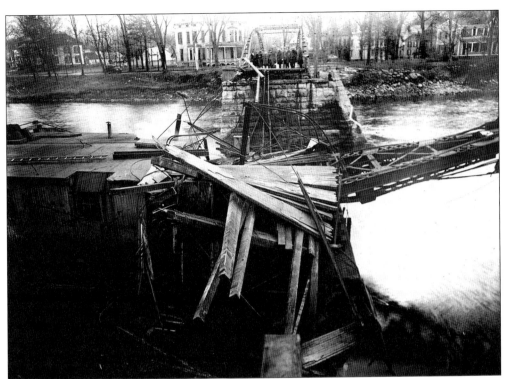

On November 23, 1922, a Barge Canal dredge destroyed part of the Mohawk River bridge at Fonda and Fultonville. From the Fultonville side of the river, people watch as the barge smashes through the bridge.

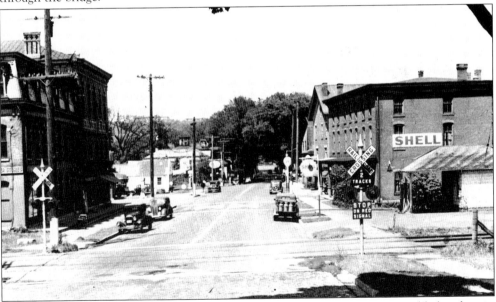

This view of Fultonville, looking north toward the Mohawk River, was most likely taken in the 1930s. The village's landscape was virtually reconstructed in the early 1950s, as numerous buildings were removed or demolished in preparation for construction of the New York State Thruway.

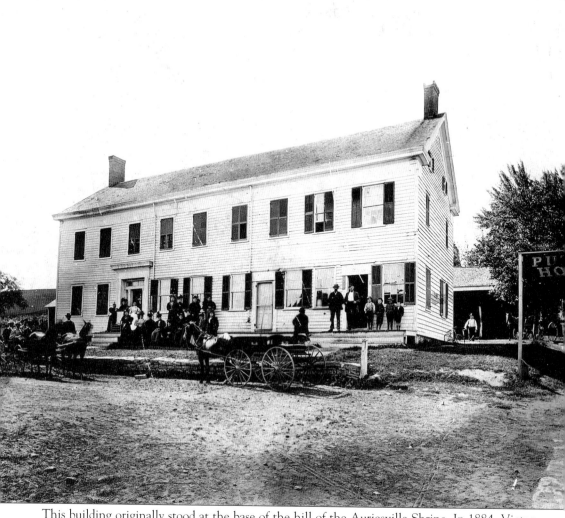

This building originally stood at the base of the hill of the Auriesville Shrine. In 1884, Victor Putman purchased it from Isaiah Montaney and moved it 800 yards to the east. There, it opened as the Putman House Hotel. Its close proximity to the Erie Canal allowed many travelers accommodations. By 1900, it had been sold to the Auriesville Shrine, which used it as lodging for its visitors. The building was razed in the 1980s, after business had been declining for a number of years.

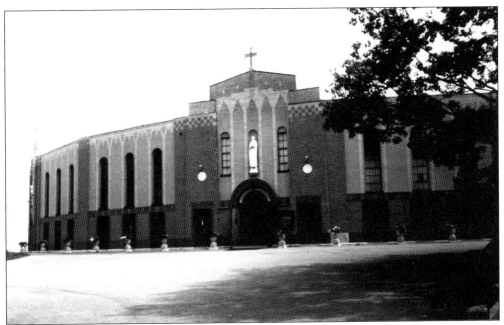

The Shrine of the North American Martyrs, better known to Montgomery County residents as the Auriesville Shrine, is located on the site of the lower Mohawk castle, Ossernenon. Here, French missionary Isaac Jogues was martyred by the Mohawks in 1646. The Coliseum, erected in 1931, is one-tenth mile in circumference and has 72 doors. Capable of seating 6,500 people, the Coliseum comfortably accommodates the thousands making annual pilgrimages to the Auriesville Shrine.

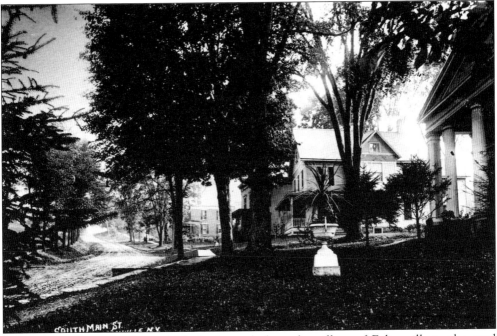

South Main Street, or Route 30A, leads south from the village of Fultonville to the rural crossroads hamlet of Glen.

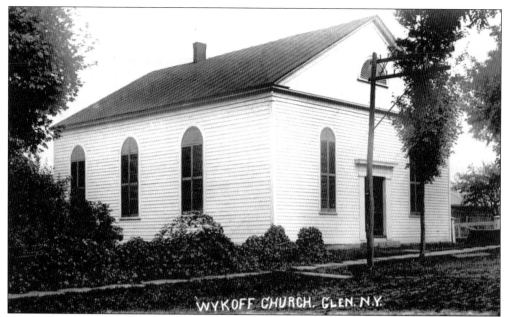

This building was constructed in 1831 to house the meetings of the "Wyckoffites," a group who, under Rev. Henry Wycoff, separated from the Glen Dutch Reformed Church and organized the True Reformed Dutch Church. The structure now serves as the Glen Reformed Church Community Hall.

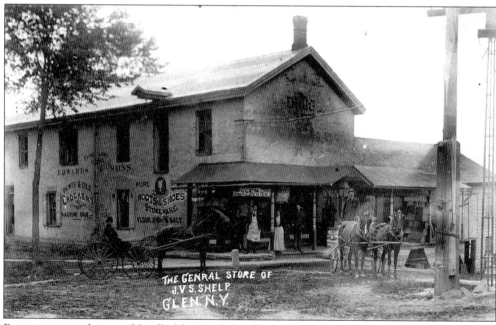

Prominent merchant and landholder Jacob Sanders Glen built the general store in the hamlet of Glen in 1818. The store was later owned by J. V. S. Edwards and then by Shelp. The two-and-a-half-story brick building, located at one of the five corners of the heavily traveled crossroads, housed the hamlet's first post office, in 1823. A fire of suspicious origin destroyed the structure in 2000. (Courtesy of Lois Gruner.)

Before the centralization of the school districts in the 1950s, each town had a number of one-room schoolhouses for its school-aged children to attend. Winne School District No. 6 was located on Argersinger Road. Built in 1848 on land leased to the trustees by Stephen Ostrom for 1¢ a year, the structure has been renovated and converted into a private residence.

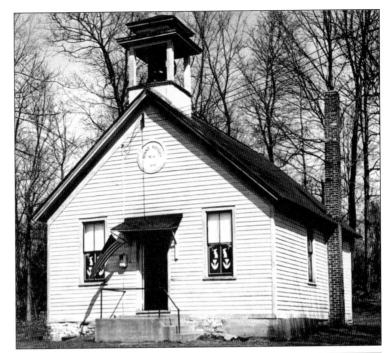

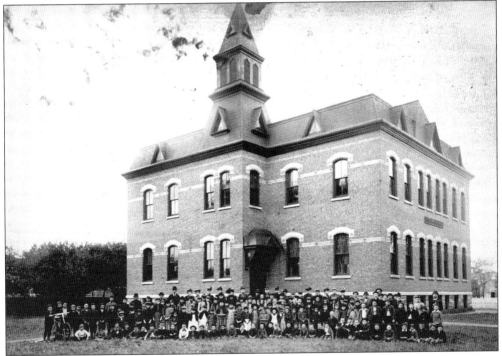

Constructed in 1884, the Fultonville Union Free School faced Union Street. In charge were D. L. Lehman, principal; Miss Jones, assistant principal; Miss Phillips, intermediate grades teacher; and Miss C. Kibbe, primary grades teacher. This picture was taken on October 22, 1891. The building burned on January 8, 1923, the first day of school after Christmas vacation. Today, a park and a historical marker erected by the school's alumni are all that remain on the site.

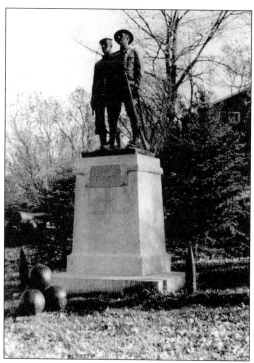

"Like Hell They Can!" The Soldiers and Sailors Monument represents the doughboy and sailor of World War I as they stand with courage against the enemy. The bronze memorial, sculpted by New York City's Sally James Farnham, was commissioned by the bequest of Glen native James H. Starin. State Sen. William T. Byrne, also a native of Montgomery County, addressed the 2,000 attendees at the unveiling ceremony on July 16, 1927.

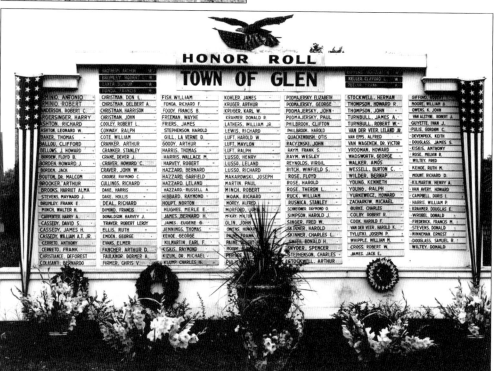

The Glen and Fultonville World War II Honor Roll was dedicated on December 1, 1944. Many of the county's villages and townships followed suit, honoring the soldiers that went off to war. By 1946, the War Department had accounted for 175 army casualties from Montgomery County.

Six

MINDEN

With the division of the town of Canajoharie on March 2, 1798, almost 33,000 acres of land was organized to form the town of Minden, so called by the German settlers remembering their homeland. Bounded on the west by Herkimer County and on the east by Canajoharie, Minden has, over the years, revealed evidence of Native American settlements throughout the area. The Otsquago Creek is the principal stream.

The center of early activity occurred at Sand Hill, in the northwestern section of Minden. In addition to stores and a trading post, the Reformed church, built at Sand Hill in 1761, was clearly visible from the nearby military outpost, Fort Plain, erected in 1776.

By the 1830s, settlement moved east to the present village of Fort Plain. Incorporated as a village in 1832, the growing community took its name from the then defunct fortification. The county's first newspaper, the *Watchtower*, began publication in Fort Plain in 1827. A toll bridge was constructed across the Mohawk River, linking Fort Plain to Nelliston. Tolls were lifted after 1857.

For many years, Minden's industry was characterized by agriculture, carriage and furniture companies, and knitting mills. Freysbush, Fordsbush, Mindenville, and Keesler's Corners are among Minden's hamlets.

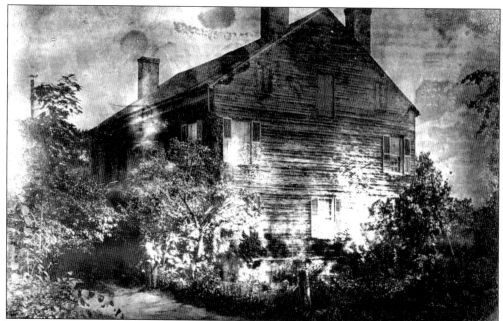

Currently owned and used by the Fort Plain chapter of the Daughters of the American Revolution, the Isaac Paris house is a remnant of the post–Revolutionary Colonial period. Constructed by Isaac Paris Jr. in 1786, the building was used as a residence and trading post. Paris was honored when settlers in present Oneida County named their town after him; he had saved them from virtual starvation with shipments of grain in 1789. (Courtesy of Sandra Cronkhite, Fort Plain historian.)

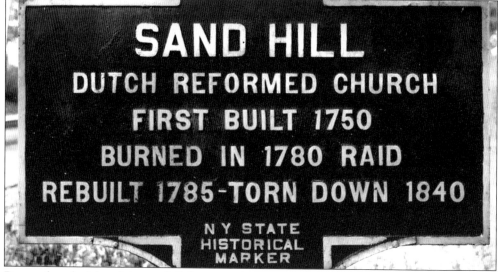

Due to the ethnicity of the area's Palatine settlers, services at the Sand Hill Church were given in German. From the west side of the Dutchtown Road site, congregation members had a good view of Fort Plain, garrisoned to defend the area during the Revolutionary War. After Rev. John I. Wack was dismissed from the Montgomery Classis (for drunkenness, insubordination, and delving too deeply into the private lives of his parishioners), services were transferred to the village, where a new structure was built.

Services for the Methodist congregation were first held in Fort Plain in 1832. Before constructing a church, members met on the second floor of a building on Canal Street. Meetings were also held in the schoolhouse. The first house of worship built for the congregation was the wood-framed structure seen here. Constructed in 1845, the building was enlarged and rededicated in 1854. The church was taken down 25 years later and was replaced with the current brick edifice.

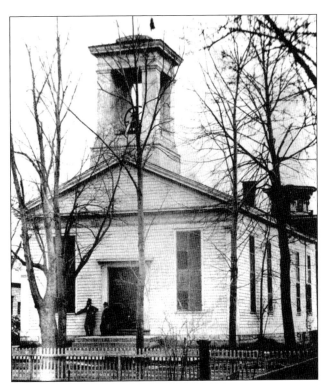

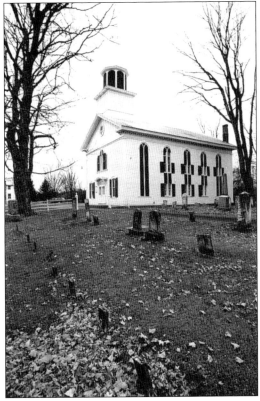

The Freysbush Methodist Church and Cemetery, located off Route 163, have a quaint rural setting. Built in 1828 on land donated by John Diefendorf, the church was completely renovated in 1870. Church trustees divided the adjoining cemetery into lots in 1840, reserving a special section for the Black members of the congregation.

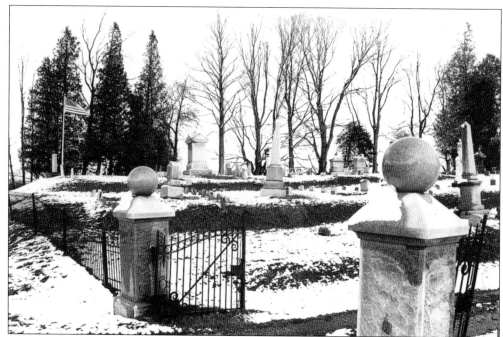

Mount Hope Cemetery is a testament to the organization of the Evangelical Lutheran church in the hamlet of Fordsbush. The cemetery was incorporated 25 years after the construction of the church. Rev. Nicholas Van Alstine (1814–1900), pastor at the church, was a diligent advocate for abolishing slavery, consistently attacking the practice in his writings to the Lutheran Synod and from the pulpit.

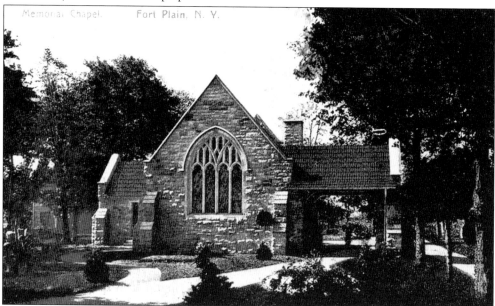

The Fort Plain Cemetery sits upon a hill in the northwest corner of the village. The cemetery association was organized in 1864 to oversee the vast final resting place for many residents. Mrs. H. H. Benedict donated the stone memorial chapel in 1907 in honor of her mother, Catherine Nellis.

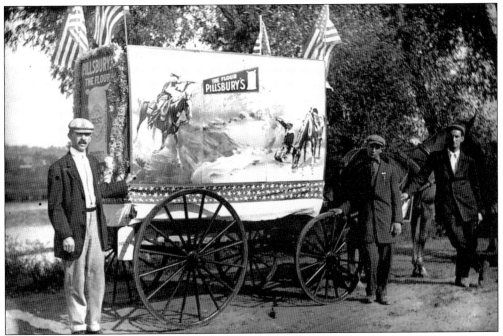

Pillsbury flour was delivered to Fort Plain residents by, from left to right, Charles Z. Brandow, an unidentified man, and Jay Gobel. (Courtesy of Sandra Cronkhite, Fort Plain historian.)

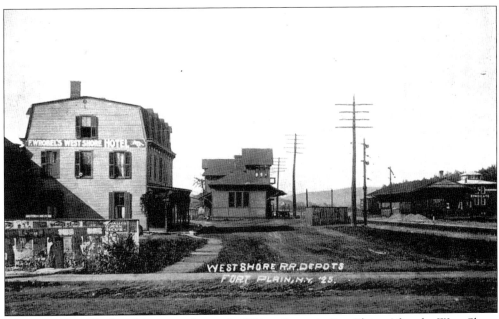

The West Shore Railroad depot was located off River Street in Fort Plain. After the West Shore was absorbed into the New York Central Railroad, freight, rather than passengers, passed through the station. (Courtesy of Sandra Cronkhite, Fort Plain historian.)

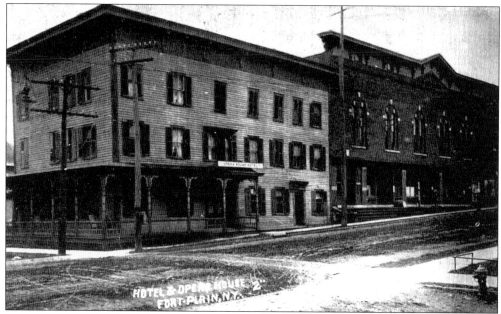

The Fritcher Opera House was built in 1878 on River Street north of the canal. Numerous events, such as the benefit for the Clinton Liberal Institute Athletic Association (held in 1900, one month after the academic institution burned down), took place here. In 1911, this building and the adjacent Union Hotel were destroyed by fire. The property was purchased and donated to the village by Frederick W. Haslett. Music continues as a part of the site, with summer concerts in the Haslett Park bandstand. (Courtesy of Sandra Cronkhite, Fort Plain historian.)

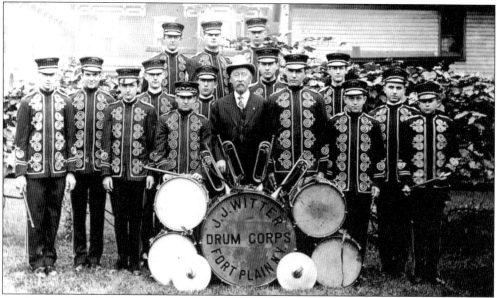

Bands played a significant role in the cultural lives of many Montgomery County residents in the late 1890s and early 1990s. Fort Plain had not only the Old Fort Plain Band but also the J. J. Witter Drum and Bugle Corps. The corps was named for J. J. Witter, an English professor and Fort Plain School principal who introduced physical education to the curriculum. (Courtesy of Sandra Cronkhite, Fort Plain historian.)

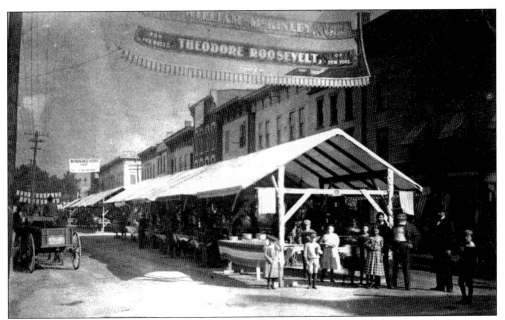

Residents enjoy the activities at the Fort Plain Street Fair in 1900. Thousands attended the fairs, viewing the exhibits lining Canal Street. Merchants set up their wares in front of their stores. Other attractions included high dives, concerts, rides, and baseball games. Note the banner announcing the campaign of William McKinley and Theodore Roosevelt for president and vice president, respectively.

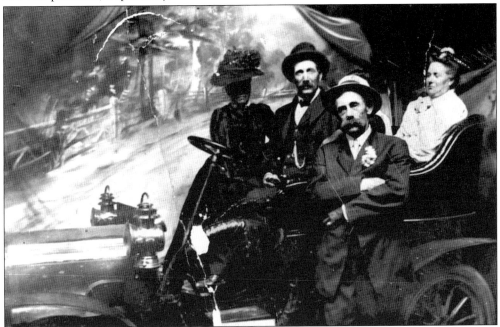

Henry Baum (second from left) and Angelina (Smith) Baum (right), along with another couple, try out the new automobile exhibit at the Fort Plain Street Fair held from September 13 to 18, 1909. The fairs were held annually, traditionally in early September, from 1898 until 1924, with the exception of the World War I years. (Author's collection.)

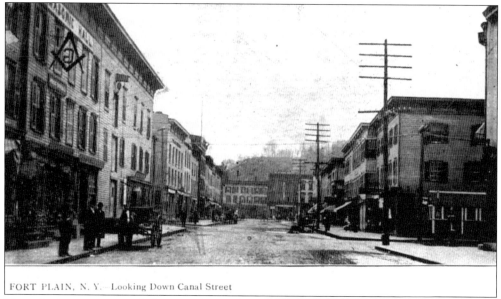

FORT PLAIN, N. Y. — Looking Down Canal Street

Many businesses occupied the storefronts along Canal Street c. 1900. Today, the scenery reveals a vastly different view, as all of the businesses have changed. (Courtesy of Sandra Cronkhite, Fort Plain historian.)

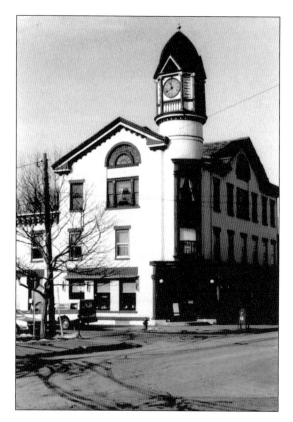

Located at the corner of Canal and Mohawk Streets in Fort Plain, the Clock Building is a notable structure. Constructed in 1832, the square building, originally known as Montgomery Hall, was operated as a leading hotel in the valley. Later the Farmers & Mechanics Bank, the building acquired a clock in the late 1800s. A policeman or bank trustee was given the task of winding the clock. Eventually, the clock was converted to electric.

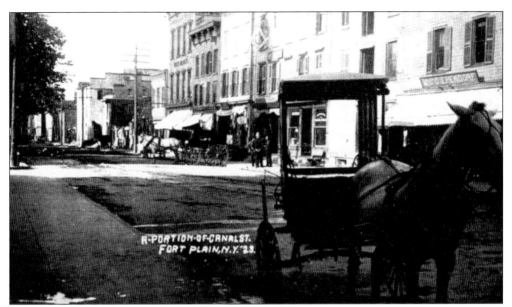

Canal Street, with a horse-and-buggy, is pictured here before it was paved. During the first half of the 20th century, Fort Plain experienced a period of great development. Nearly all of the streets were paved, and concrete sidewalks and a storm sewer system were installed. Canal Street was paved from Main to Orchard, along with a number of other avenues, in 1904. (Courtesy of Sandra Cronkhite, Fort Plain historian.)

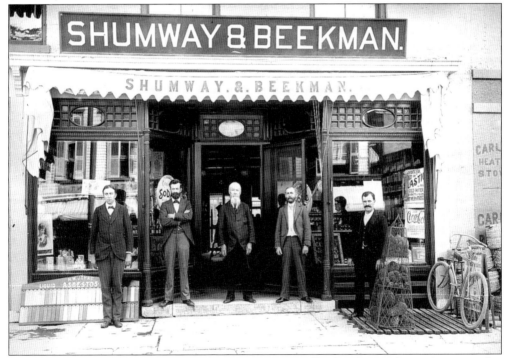

Walter F. Shumway, a native of nearby Van Hornesville (Herkimer County), operated a drugstore at 46 Canal Street for many years. He partnered with Devoe and then Beekman and then went on his own sometime before 1928.

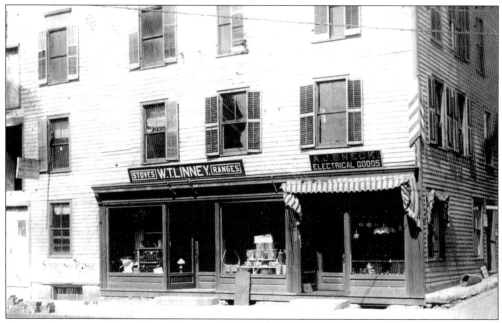

As in other area villages, Fort Plain's early growth and prosperity can be attributed to traffic on the Erie Canal. W. T. Linney and A. J. Sneck operated stores on the corner of Canal and River Streets. Julius Failing, an electrician who was self-taught through correspondence courses, worked for Sneck, whose business was responsible for electrifying most of Fort Plain and Nelliston.

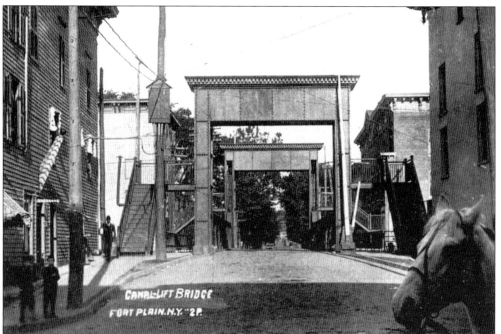

Lift bridges across the Erie Canal allowed access to the businesses on Fort Plain's Canal Street. This particular iron lift bridge replaced the former wooden bridge that collapsed in the late 1890s as a drove of cattle and a omnibus full of passengers tried to cross the bridge at the same time.

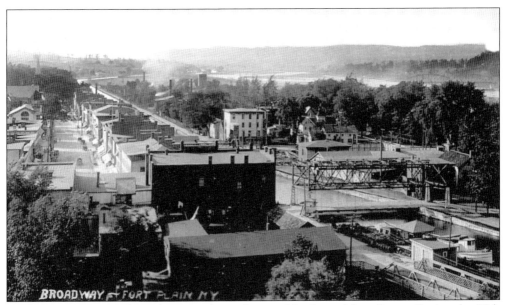

Looking west at Fort Plain, this view shows the canal bridge at Main Street. During the 19th century, Minden's population steadily increased. In the 20th century, however, the town's population experienced fluctuations, decreasing by six percent from 1990 to 2000. (Courtesy of Sandra Cronkhite, Fort Plain historian.)

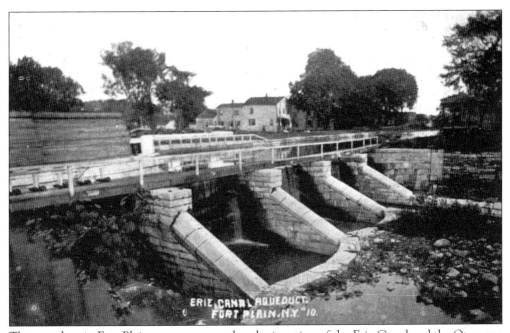

The aqueduct in Fort Plain was constructed at the junction of the Erie Canal and the Otsquago Creek on State Street. The limestone structure, a quiet reminder of the village's hustle and bustle during the days of the canal, was destroyed on October 28, 1981, after torrential rains flooded the Otsquago Creek. Rushing water, trees, and debris proved too much for the landmark to hold back. (Courtesy of Sandra Cronkhite, Fort Plain historian.)

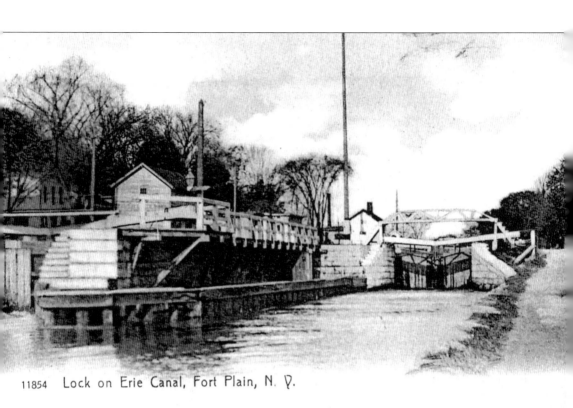

11854 Lock on Erie Canal, Fort Plain, N. Y.

Passengers and cargo, transported along the Erie Canal, passed through Lock No. 32 in the eastern part of Fort Plain. Travelers were able to purchase general merchandise at the canal store in the Lockville section of the village. The lock was doubled in 1827, and property owners along the canal submitted claims to the state for any damages or expenses incurred during the enlargement of the canal in the late 1830s and early 1840s.

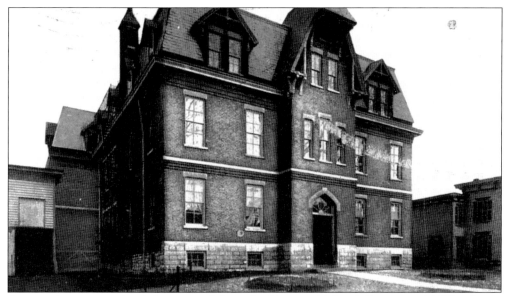

Area students were schooled at a wood-frame building on Mohawk Street until 1879, when a brick building was erected on the site. By 1893, the school had united with the Lockville section school. This building then became the high school, with primary and grammar departments. After a new school was constructed at the former Clinton Liberal Institute location, the Masons purchased the building, which they continue to use as their meeting place. In need of space again after World War II, the school district briefly rented rooms for classes. (Courtesy of Lois Gruner.)

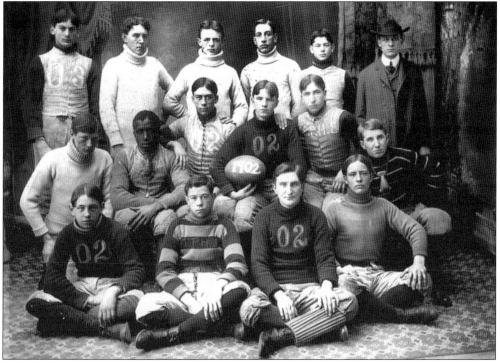

The 1902 Fort Plain High School football team is pictured here.

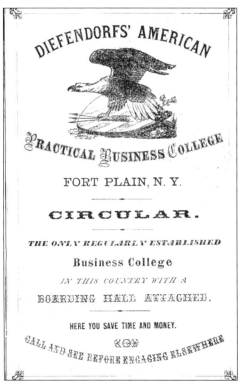

Rev. Benjamin I. Diefendorf, minister of the Universalist church, also served as principal of the Fort Plain Seminary. His son, A. Benson C. Diefendorf, was a professor of penmanship. The Diefendorf American Practical Business College operated only a few years between the closing of the Fort Plain Seminary and the opening of the Clinton Liberal Institute.

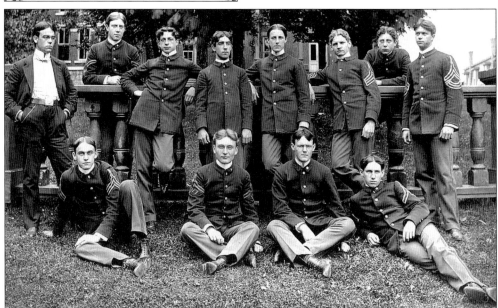

The Clinton Liberal Institute moved from Clinton to Fort Plain in 1879. The building was enlarged and the armory was built in 1890, when the school added military instruction. During its peak, the institute had an enrollment of 200 students, among them Simon Lake, inventor of the submarine. Although it remained a coeducational school for most of its tenure, the institute limited its education to males just prior to being destroyed by fire on March 25, 1900.

Seven

MOHAWK

Formed as a township on April 4, 1837, Mohawk was part of Tryon County's original Mohawk District, which covered both sides of the Mohawk River. Currently, the township is bounded on the south by the river, the north by Fulton County, the west by Palatine, and the east by Amsterdam. The Cayadutta Creek, the town's principal stream, empties into the Mohawk River.

Early settlers included the Hansens, Butlers, Collinses, and Veeders, as well as the Douw Fonda family, arriving from Schenectady in 1751. The Dutch settlement of Caughnawaga was at the eastern limits of the present Fonda village. The raising of the liberty pole at Caughnawaga in May 1775 and the ensuing confrontation between some 300 patriots and Loyalists Guy and John Johnson, overruled any authority the Johnsons had had over Mohawk Valley residents. The event was the valley's first bloodshed of the Revolution.

Fonda, incorporated in 1851, became the county seat in 1836, when the Montgomery County Board of Supervisors decided to move county business away from Johnstown to be closer to the railroad and the Erie Canal. The Old Courthouse is one of the finest examples of Ionic architecture in the Mohawk Valley, if not the state.

Milk, cheese, hops, and broomcorn were significant agricultural crops through the years.

The Fonda, Johnstown, & Gloversville Railroad steam and trolley lines, affectionately known as "the Huckleberry," connecting Fonda to the North Country, were a significant business venture lasting close to a century.

The hamlets of Mohawk are Berryville (along the Cayadutta Creek), Yosts, and Tribes Hill.

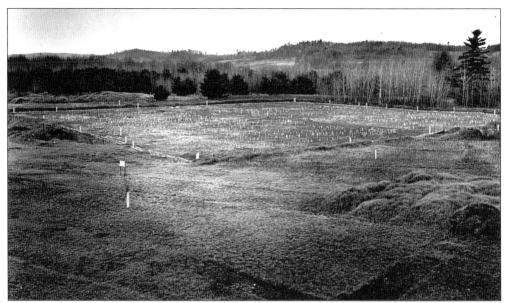

When the French destroyed the Native American village of Ossernenon, the residents moved to the north side of the river and built their new village, Caughnawaga, above the present village of Fonda. Kateri Tekakwitha, "the Lily of the Mohawks," lived in this village for a time before her trek to Canada and after embracing Christianity in 1676. The Caughnawaga site has been excavated to reveal the post holes for the longhouse walls and the palisaded walls around the village.

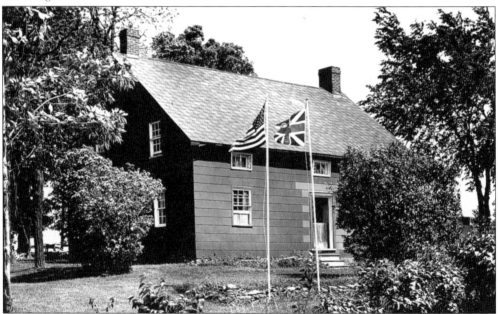

Butlersbury, built by Walter Butler in 1742, is a good example of Colonial architecture. The Butlers, occupying the home for three generations, were infamous Loyalists and participants in Johnson's raids throughout the Mohawk and Schoharie Valleys. Confiscated after the war, Butlersbury is a rare vestige of the Revolutionary War period. The original beams and wood floors remain in the now private residence.

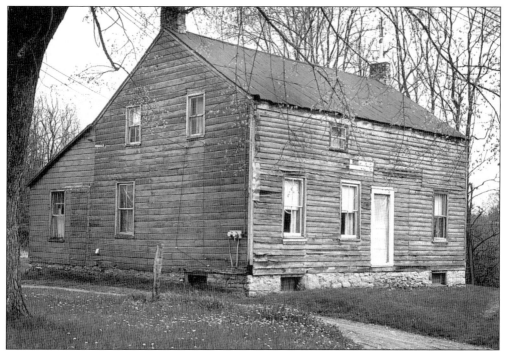

Peggy Wemple, daughter of Fonda's early settler Douw Fonda, operated a tavern during the Revolutionary War. Wemple's patriotic bravery resonated throughout the valley, as she did not give in to intimidation when a dead Native American was hung in the doorway of her tavern. The house, built in 1780 near the Cayadutta Creek, stood until 1997.

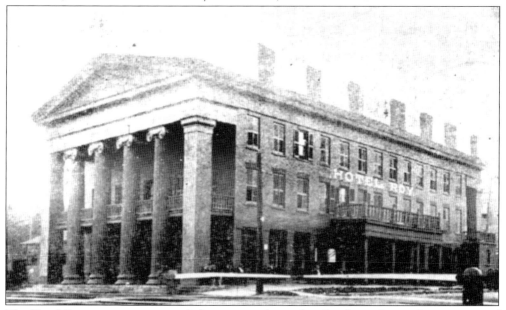

The Hotel Roy, as it was commonly known, was located in Fonda on the southwest corner of Main and Broadway. Constructed on the site of the old stage house in 1836, the hotel closely resembled the courthouse just across the tracks of the New York Central Railroad. The original 25 large sleeping quarters and third-floor ballroom were later converted into 40 lodging rooms.

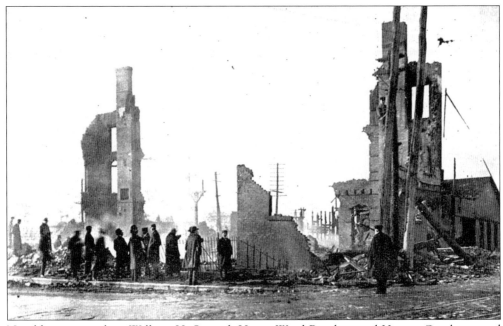

Notable guests such as William H. Seward, Henry Ward Beecher, and Horace Greeley stayed at Fonda's Hotel Roy before it was destroyed by fire on the cold, wintry afternoon of January 25, 1909. The hotel proprietors had allegedly hired an arsonist for a portion of the insurance money. Although all of the guests fled the scene unharmed, night watchman John McMaster died from the injuries he sustained while trying to escape.

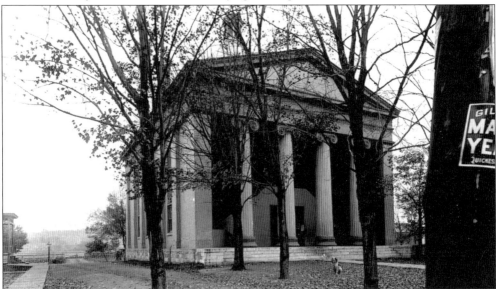

An important reminder of Montgomery County's history, the Old Courthouse signifies the arrival of the county seat in Fonda in 1836, due to the proximity to the railroad and the Erie Canal. Numerous cases were tried in the splendid Greek Revival edifice, including a few murder trials and a libel case involving noted author James Fenimore Cooper. Retaining its magnificence after more than 160 years, the Old Courthouse is home to the Montgomery County Department of History and Archives.

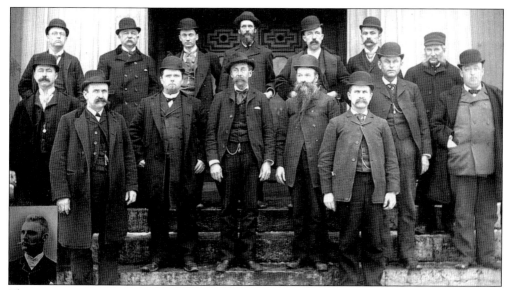

The Montgomery County Board of Supervisors gathers on the front steps of the Old Courthouse in 1892. From left to right are the following: (first row) Patrick Doorey, fourth ward; Simon R. Bulger, Minden; James Doak, second ward; John P. Hall, Charleston; Seely Conover, first ward; William Clark, Amsterdam; John V. Putman, Glen; and E. S. J. Hand, Amsterdam; (second row) J. E. Willoughby, clerk; W. N. Johnson, Palatine; Ed J. Perkins, fifth ward; C. W. Scudder, chairman, St. Johnsville; A. A. Lyker, Root; James W. Dygert, Canajoharie; and George Jones, Mohawk. Pictured in the lower left is Robert M. Hartley, Florida.

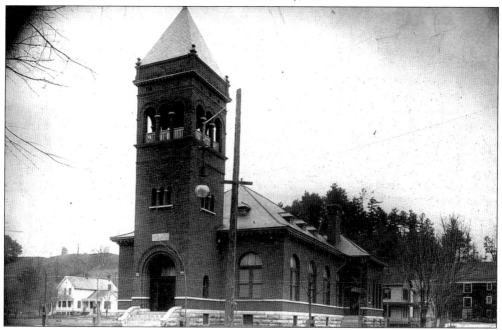

Ironically, one of the factors that had attracted county officials to the site of the Old Courthouse—the railroad—became a hindrance, as the excessive noise disrupted proceedings. This new courthouse was constructed far enough away from the din of railroad, and additions to it were built in 1940, 1962, and 1988.

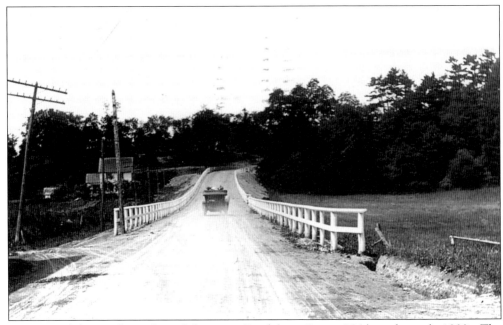

An automobile travels north on Johnstown Road (now Route 30A) in the early 1900s. The Montgomery County Office Building was constructed on the flats to the right of the road in 1965. Today, houses line the left side of the road.

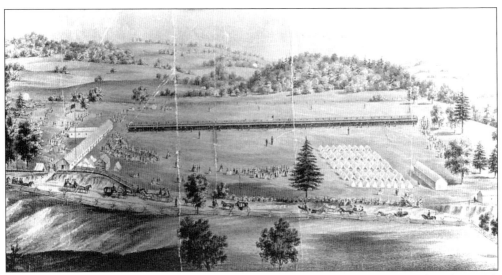

Camp Mohawk sat upon a hill off the Johnstown Road on the outskirts of Fonda. The 115th and 153rd Regiments of the New York State Volunteers mustered in and trained for battle here. Col. Simeon Sammons, commander of the 115th, lived on Johnstown Road, a few miles north of Camp Mohawk. All that remains is a historical marker designating the approximate location of the encampment.

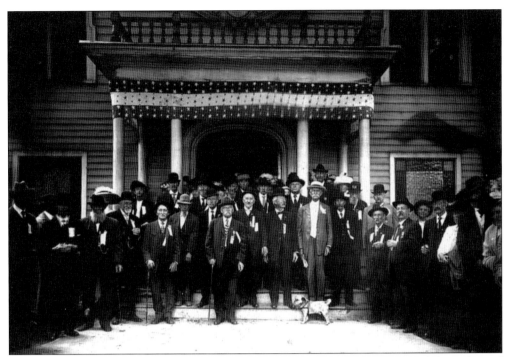

Veterans of the 115th and 153rd New York State Volunteers pose on the steps of the Reformed church on the 50th anniversary (August 26, 1912) of the 115th's departure from Camp Mohawk to the front lines of the Civil War.

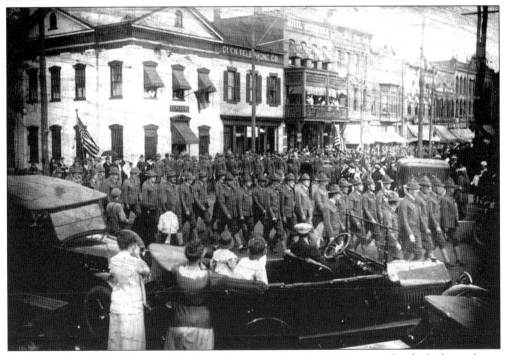

On September 22, 1917, many Fonda residents watch on Main Street as the drafted men leave to enter World War I.

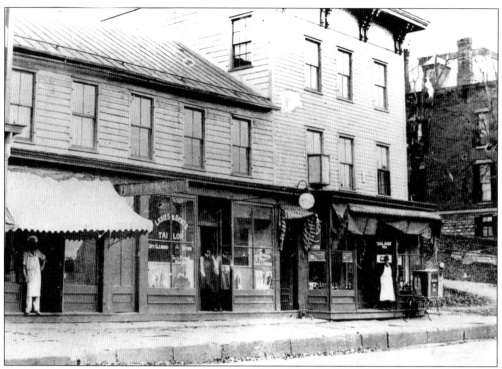

Frank Ruzicka, baker (left), Frank Banowicz, tailor (center), and Joe Conte, grocer, stand in front of their shops in 1922. This block of buildings, on the northwest corner of Main and Center Streets in Fonda, burned in 1926. Today, a Cumberland Farms store occupies the site.

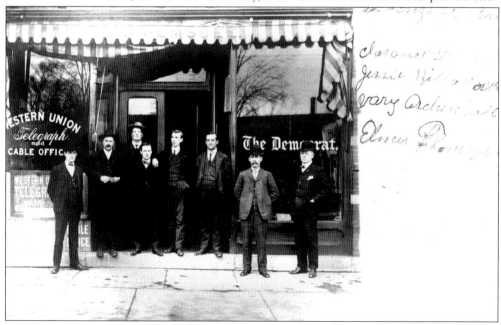

Men stand in front of the Western Union and *Mohawk Valley Democrat* offices. First published as the *Fonda Herald*, the *Mohawk Valley Democrat* was considered the oldest weekly newspaper in Montgomery County until rising production costs forced its closing in 1990.

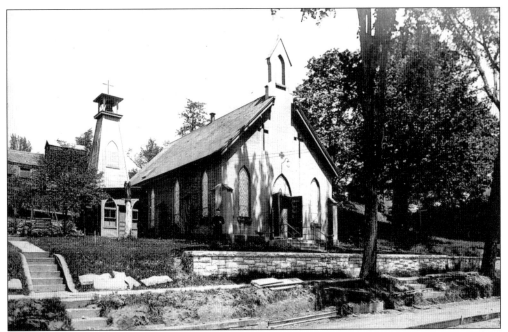

Although the first Catholic services held in Mohawk were at St. Peter's Chapel in the Indian village of Caughnawaga, a Catholic congregation was not established until 1882. This first St. Cecelia's Church, on Main Street, acted as a mission for St. Patrick's Church in Johnstown. Services were held here until 1923, when the congregation outgrew the building, which for a number of years then served as the American Legion Floyd Deckro Post No. 383.

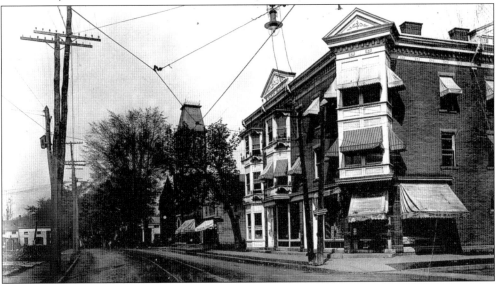

This view of West Main Street in Fonda shows the Methodist church, the post office, and the drugstore. Itinerant minister Rev. P. Moriarity preached a sermon at the courthouse in 1842, which led to the beginnings of the Methodist congregation in Fonda. The church's rapidly increasing membership outgrew the first structure, and a second was constructed in 1843. On April 12, 1912, fire broke out in Briggs's Drug Store, spreading to the post office and John Davis's newsstand on the east and to the Methodist church on the west.

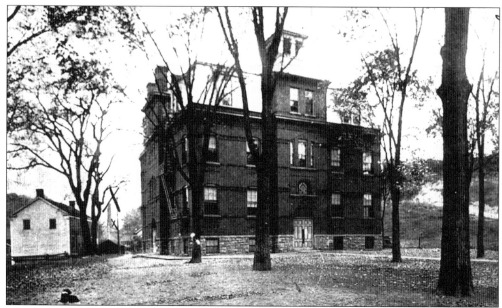

This three-story brick building was constructed in 1886 to replace the former decaying schoolhouse and was established as a Union Free School the following year. It had become a high school by 1897, with a first graduating class of just four students. The last class graduated in 1938. Kasson & Keller purchased the building and constructed the factory's walls around the structure.

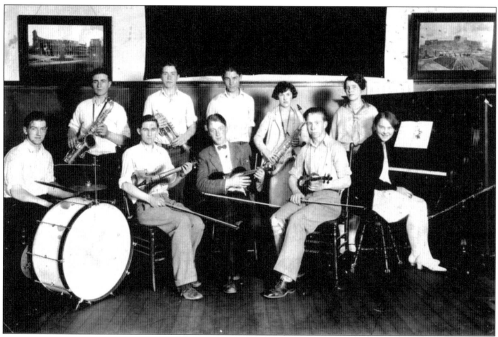

The 1928 Fonda High School band poses for a picture. From left to right are the following: (first row) John Jackson, drums; Jim Glen, first violin; Frank Rogers, second violin; Millard Crane, third violin; and Betty Burch, piano; (second row) Andrew Papa, saxophone; Dever Crane, cornet; Alfred Burch; Helen Perry, saxophone; and Margaret Vedder Drake.

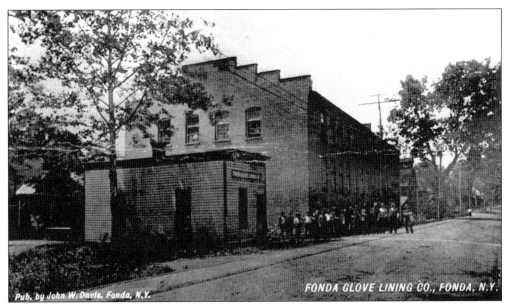

Lucius Littauer, manufacturer of wool and cotton lining and fleeces, incorporated the Fonda Glove Lining Company in 1902. Later known as the Fonda Manufacturing Company, the Cayadutta Street business was one of Fonda's leading industries until it was destroyed by fire on October 26, 1976.

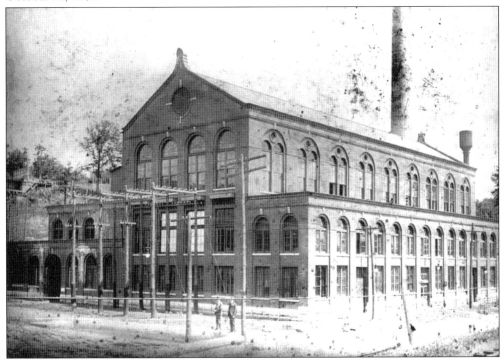

The powerhouse in Tribes Hill supplied electricity to the extensive Fonda, Johnstown, & Gloversville trolley system. The steam-driven plant supplied 13,000 volts to three substations at Glenville, Amsterdam, and Johnstown. Also a source of power for the city of Amsterdam, the powerhouse became obsolete when the trolley lines were replaced by motorbuses in the 1930s.

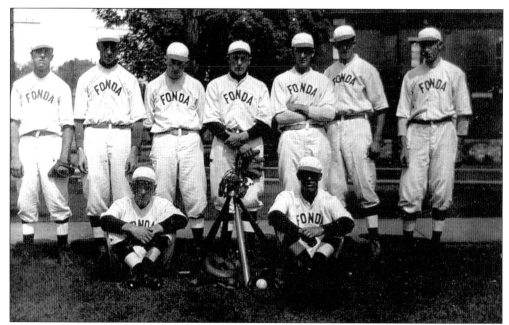

This is the Fonda baseball team of 1919. From left to right are the following: (first row) Robert Fonda, right field; and Arthur Andrews, second base; (second row) Ira Wilson, pitcher; Paul Quick, catcher; William Ryan, third base; Ralph MacLaughlin, shortstop; Richard Furkhart, center field; Ralph Kurlbaum, left field; and Granville Quick, first base. Not pictured are Richard Furkhart, manager, and Abe Brand, umpire. The team ended with a record of 17 wins and 8 losses that year.

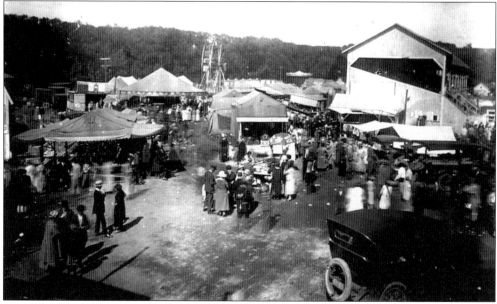

The Montgomery County Agricultural Society first organized in 1844 and purchased the present grounds of 13 acres in 1863. In addition to the county-wide fair, the society sponsored other events at the fairgrounds such as rodeos, Barnum & Bailey's Circus (in 1894), and car races with nationally recognized drivers such as Shirley "Cha Cha" Muldowney and Kyle Petty.

Eight

PALATINE

On March 7, 1788, Palatine was formed as a township from the Tryon County district of the same name. The original size of the township was drastically reduced with the separation and formation of Salisbury in 1797 (now in Herkimer County), Oppenheim in 1808, and Ephratah in 1827 (both in Fulton County). Today, the township is bound on the south by the Mohawk River, the north by Fulton County, the east by Mohawk, and the west by St. Johnsville.

Receiving its name from the Palatine Germans who came to the area with the Stone Arabia Patent in 1723, Palatine welcomed early settler Heinrich Frey. Frey emigrated from Switzerland *c.* 1690 and settled along the Mohawk River in present Palatine Bridge, running a trading post. His son is believed to have been the first white child born west of Schenectady.

Palatine Church, known earlier as Fox's Mills, was the town's largest settlement in the early 1800s, with 35 dwellings, several stores, and the stone Lutheran church. Stone Arabia, the area covered by the patent, included two churches, two hotels, a cheese factory, and a dozen farmhouses.

The township's two villages, Palatine Bridge and Nelliston, were incorporated in 1867 and 1878, respectively. The bridge built in 1798 across the river at Palatine Bridge to Canajoharie connected the north and south sides of the county and was the first river bridge constructed west of Schenectady. The New York Central Railroad line ran through both of these communities.

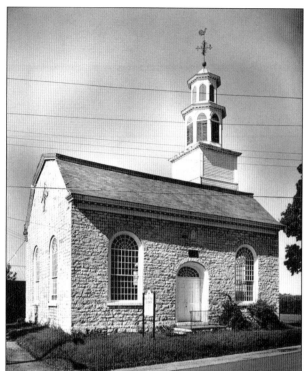

Built in 1770 on the King's Highway, with donations from numerous local families, the Palatine Church escaped destruction during the October 19, 1780, raid when a Loyalist member of the Nellis family requested that it be spared. The Nellis family was among those who had contributed toward the church's construction.

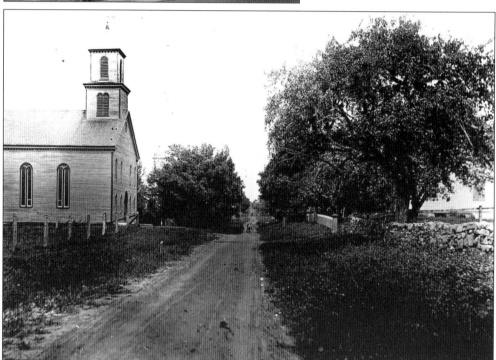

The Lutheran Trinity Church occupies the site of the original log church that was destroyed by Sir John Johnson's army during the October 19, 1780, Battle of Stone Arabia. The present church was erected in 1792.

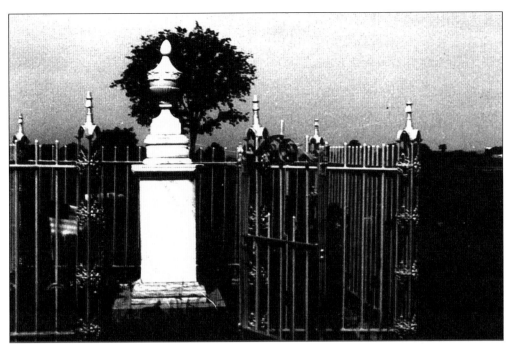

In a small cemetery behind the Stone Arabia's Reformed Dutch Church is the grave of Col. John Brown. On October 19, 1780, Brown and a militia of 200 fought against Sir John Johnson's forces in an open field. The combined strength of British troops, Loyalists, and Native Americans proved too much for the smaller army, which lost about 30 of its number, including the colonel.

The Reformed Dutch Church in Stone Arabia, located just north of the Lutheran Trinity Church, was constructed in 1788, after the first building was destroyed in the 1780 battle. Relatively few changes have been made to the Georgian-style structure over the years—the major alteration being the closing of the entrance on the east side. Rev. B. B. Westfall, pastor of the congregation, is buried under the pulpit.

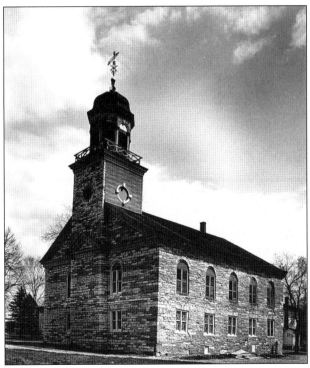

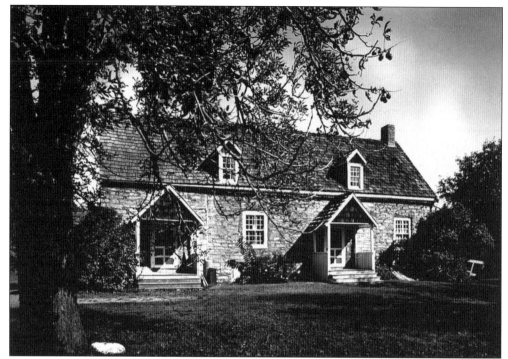

Fort Frey, at the western edge of the village of Palatine Bridge, overlooking the Mohawk River, was the 1739 home of Swiss emigrant Heinrich Frey, who came to the valley *c.* 1690. The fur trader's fortified home was occupied by British troops during the French and Indian War. Today, it is a private residence.

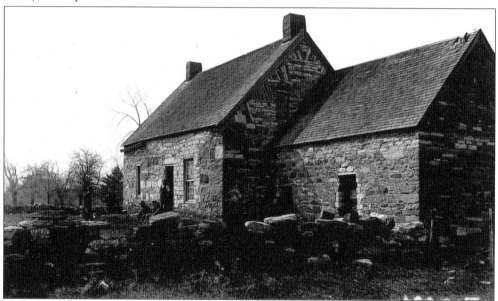

The Ehle house was an early Colonial landmark in the present village of Nelliston. It served as a mission to the Mohawk Indians of Tarajorees, the settlement located on the present Prospect Hill in Fort Plain. Rev. Johan Jacob Ehle constructed the home in 1727; the larger portion followed in 1752.

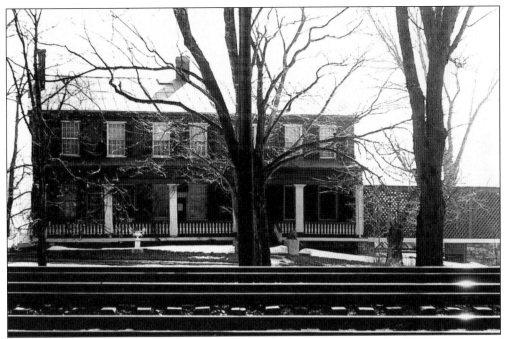

The Spraker family constructed its homestead on the north bank of the Mohawk River, east of Palatine Bridge, in 1795. A tavern on the Mohawk Turnpike, the homestead also served residents from the south side, accessible by a ferry across the river to Sprakers Basin. A one-time stop on the New York Central Railroad, the structure was razed by the Spraker family in the 1960s to prevent further damage by vandals.

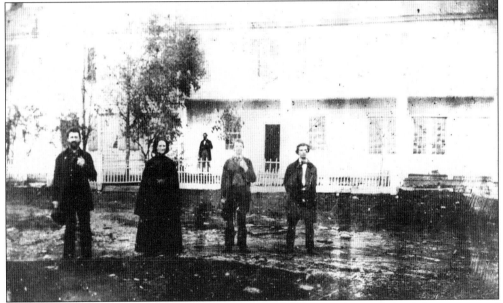

Archibald Fox stands on the porch, and Elizabeth Gros Fox and sons Roland, Lawrence, and Henry Clay Fox stand on the road opposite the Palatine Church at Fox's Tavern. A once-busy stop on the Mohawk Turnpike, Fox's Tavern also served as a post office and inn. The wide flats near the tavern were allegedly used for training of the militia

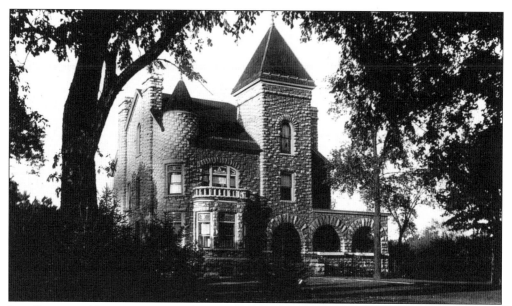

Locally quarried limestone was used to construct numerous buildings throughout Montgomery County. This example of unique architecture is located on West Grand Street (Route 5) in Palatine Bridge. It was constructed as a home for Civil War Maj. William N. Johnston in 1886. Johnston entered the quarry industry when he formed the Mohawk Valley Stone Company with partner Henry A. Shaper in 1886. The magnificent castlelike structure was used as a restaurant in recent years before becoming a private residence again.

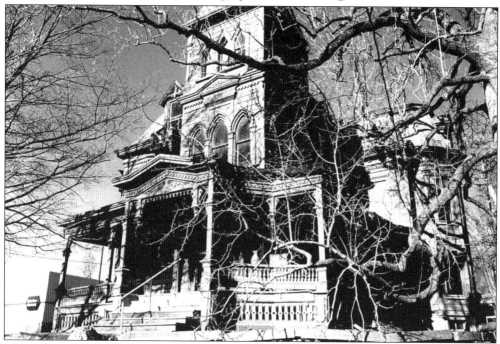

The palatial home of Webster Wagner, built just before 1868, exuded elegance throughout the Mohawk Valley, with black and French walnut interior trimmings. Born in 1817, Webster Wagner acquired his fortune by inventing the railroad sleeping car in 1858.

In addition to serving as postmaster of Palatine Bridge, Webster Wagner was elected in 1870 to the New York State Assembly and in 1874 to the New York State Senate. He served in the senate until his death in 1882. Ironically, Wagner died in one of his own palace cars in a train accident.

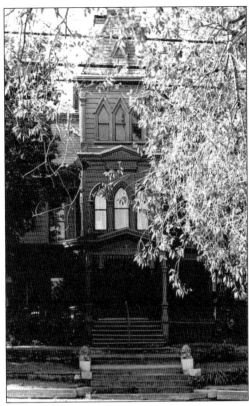

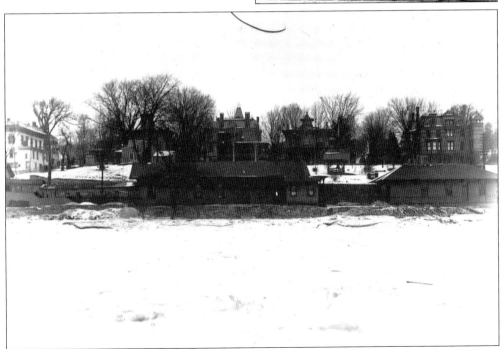

A number of the village's stately residences are visible on Grand Street above the New York Central Railroad depot in Palatine Bridge. Many of those residences have since been removed.

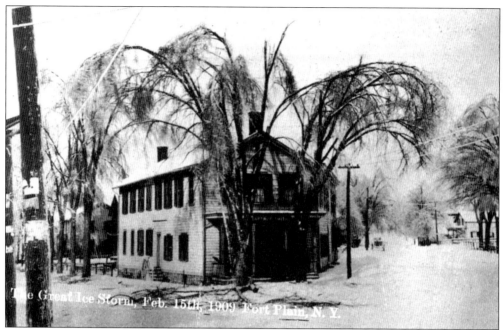

An ice storm on Feb. 15, 1909, halted traffic at the corner of West Main and Stone Arabia Streets in Nelliston. (Courtesy of Sandra Cronkhite, Fort Plain historian.)

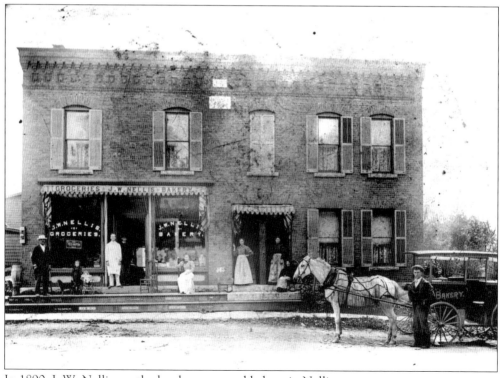

In 1890, J. W. Nellis ran the local grocery and bakery in Nelliston.

Nine

ROOT

Prior to the formation of the town of Root from Charleston and Canajoharie on January 27, 1823, settlement in that area of the county was sparse. Named for Delaware County political leader Erastus Root, the township is bounded on the north by the Mohawk River, the west by Canajoharie, the east by Glen, and the south by Charleston. Yatesville and Flat Creeks are the town's principal tributaries.

Currytown, the town's earliest settlement and first post office, took its name from the area's Corry Patent. During the Revolutionary War, residents were terrorized and murdered, and their properties were destroyed. The July 9, 1781, attack became known as the Currytown Massacre.

Rural Grove, previously known as Leatherville because of a local tannery, was so named when a prominent resident applied the identification to a letter. At one time a center of business, Rural Grove had two churches, a school, a general store, feed and sawmills, blacksmith shops, tin and cheese factories, and a hardware store.

Stone Ridge produced cobblestone for surfacing streets until that method became obsolete. Yatesville, later known as Randall, and Sprakers Basin were both stopping stations on the Erie Canal. With general stores, wagon shops, blacksmiths, insurance agencies, telegraph and post offices, and hotels, the hamlets provided everything travelers needed. Other hamlets in Root include Flat Creek, Lyker's Corners, and Brown's Hollow.

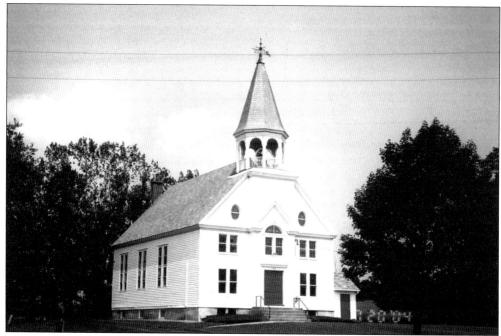

The Currytown Reformed Church congregation organized in 1790. Members met and worshiped at the home of massacre survivor Jacob Dievendorf. A church was not built until 1809. Construction of the present church structure, on Route 162, took place in 1849 at a cost of $7,500.

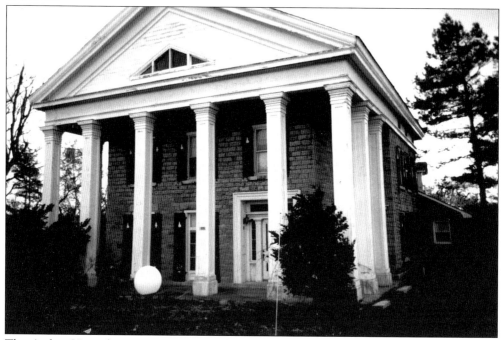

The Arthur Hayes house is a private residence on Route 162 in Currytown. The interesting stone structure is a prime example of the success of some of Root's earlier residents. (Courtesy of Lynda Z. Marino, Root historian.)

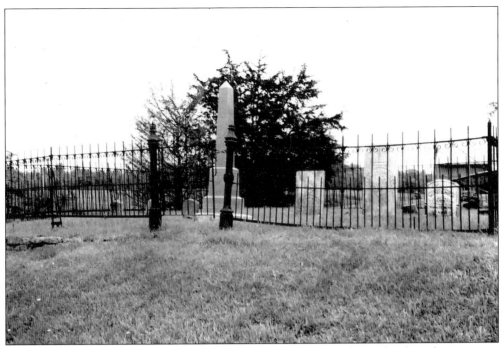

The Olmstead Cemetery is one of two graveyards on Flat Creek Road. The other contains burials of the Flanders family. (Courtesy of Lynda Z. Marino, Root historian.)

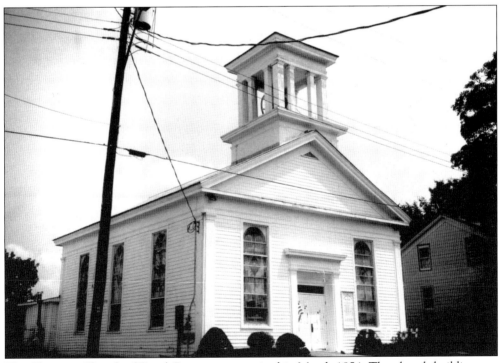

The Christian Church of Rural Grove was organized in March 1854. The church building was constructed later that summer.

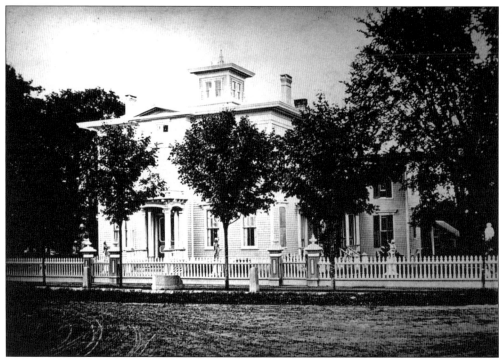

The home of John Bowdish was located near the store in Rural Grove.

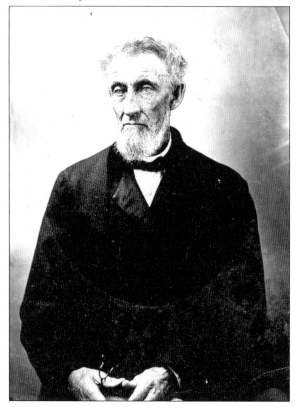

Born in 1815, John Bowdish is commonly referred to as "the Father of the Common School System" in New York State. A financier involved in a number of local banks, Bowdish strenuously advocated at the 1846 convention on education for the establishment of a free schooling system, so that everyone could have the opportunity of getting an education.

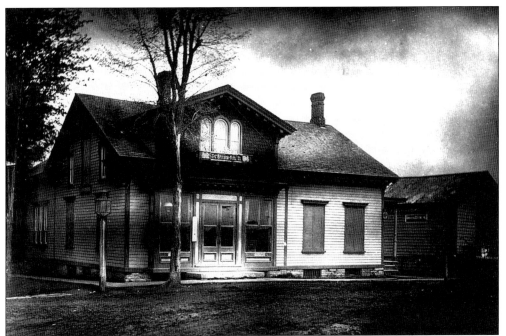

Here, the name Bowdish-Gove can still be seen above the Rural Grove Store in 1905. First started in 1829 by John Bowdish and Isaac Frost, the mercantile store came under the proprietorship of Bowdish and his son-in-law George J. Gove in 1870.

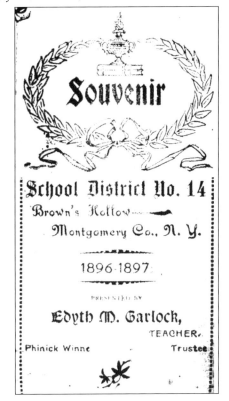

A souvenir card of Brown's Hollow School District No. 14 was given to students at the end of the 1896–1897 academic year. A second card listed the names of the teacher and students. (Courtesy of Lynda Z. Marino, Root historian.)

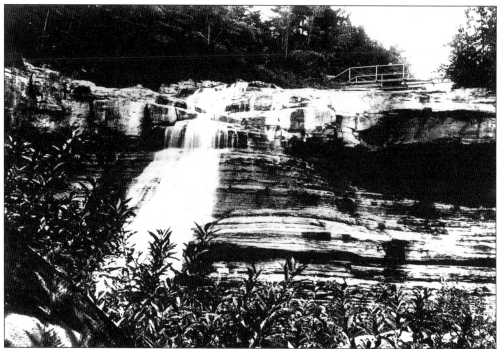

Sprakers Falls, another of Montgomery County's natural wonders, is a beautiful but dangerous sight overlooking a deep, rocky canyon.

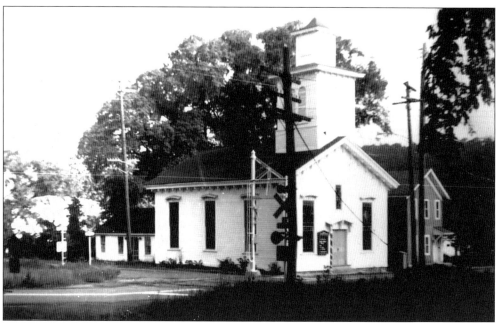

The Sprakers Reformed Church organized in 1796, with Rev. Abraham Van Horne as the first pastor. The train carrying Beech-Nut candies used to travel along the tracks past the church, and children fortunate enough to be outside at the time could catch the candy tossed to them by the train's conductor.

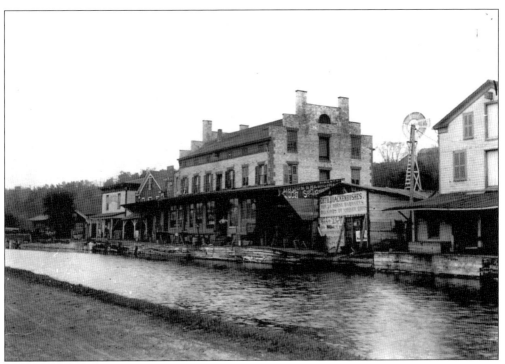

Cohen's Store, run by Silas Cohen, stood on the south bank of the Erie Canal. A post office also operated out of this building.

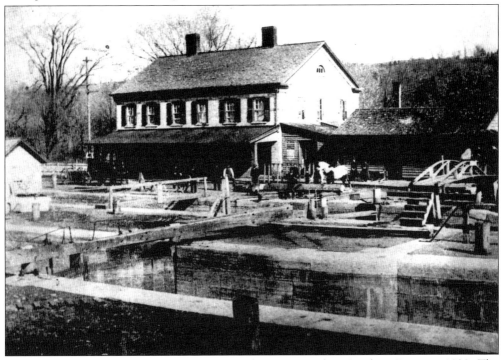

Daniel Spraker started the Spraker Store on the Erie Canal in Sprakers Basin in 1822. The warehouse accompanying the store held supplies used on the canal.

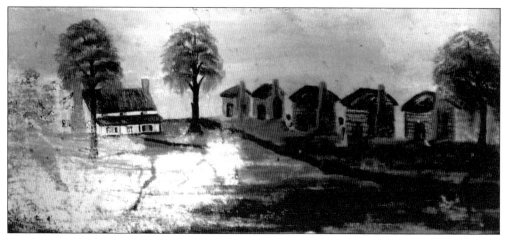

The hand-painted mural that appears in the Downing (now Maring) house is believed to represent the house and slave cabins that may have existed across the road in Randall. William H. Downing was proprietor of a canal store. He owned sheds where canal boats docked to load and unload provisions. (Courtesy of Lynda Z. Marino, Root historian.)

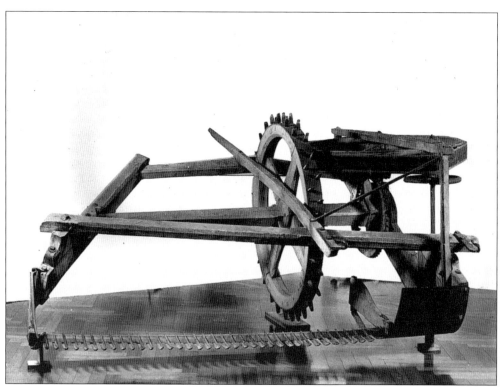

On December 23, 1834, Root resident Enoch Ambler secured a patent from Pres. Andrew Jackson for an invention with the purpose of cutting hay and grain. The primitive mowing machine was experimented on the Jacob Dievendorf farm in Currytown. Unfortunately for Ambler, he let his patent lapse and the accreditation for the revived invention went to another.

Ten

St. Johnsville

The township of St. Johnsville was created on April 28, 1838, from the town of Oppenheim, when Montgomery County was divided and Fulton County formed. Situated in the northwest corner of the county, with the Mohawk River as its southern border, St. Johnsville is bounded on the north by Fulton County and the east by Palatine. The East Canada Creek acts as a natural western boundary for St. Johnsville, separating it from Herkimer County. Zimmerman's, Crum, and Fox Creeks are other Mohawk River tributaries in the town.

The township's 11,100 acres make it the smallest town in New York State according to size.

The Palatine Germans may have settled in the township as early as 1725. The origin of the town's name is unclear, as it could have been named for surveyor Alexander St. John or possibly after the Dutch Reformed St. John's Church.

Early families were the Klocks, known for their patriotism during the Revolution, and the Zimmermans, who owned a great deal of property and established gristmills. For their prevalence in the area, the post office was first called Zimmerman's Corners. The name changed when the village was incorporated as St. Johnsville in 1857.

Development increased with the Mohawk Turnpike. Knitting mills, creameries, and shoe, piano, and agricultural tool factories were among the industries in St. Johnsville.

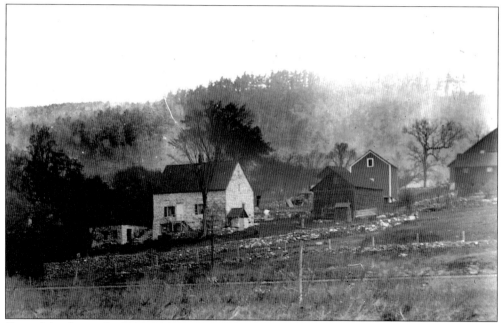

One of the few early Colonial homes remaining in Montgomery County, Fort Klock was the 1750 home and trading post of pioneer Johannes Klock. Standing on the north bank of the Mohawk River, the home was fortified to ward off attacks. The two-foot-thick walls also provided refuge for some local settlers during the Revolutionary War.

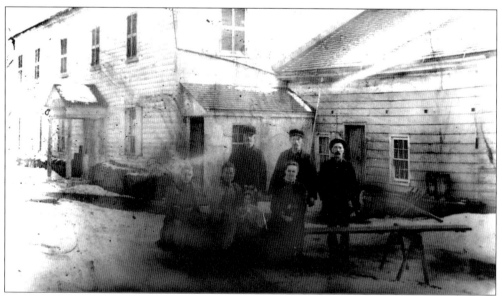

Nellis Tavern provided weary travelers along the Mohawk Turnpike with plenty of food, drink, and accommodations. Those sitting outside of the tavern may be members of the Nellis family, who owned it for a number of generations. The hostelry dates back to c. 1750, when Christian Nellis Jr. built it. Exhibiting stenciling from the early 1800s, the tavern is a rare piece of history, as it is one of a few unfortified structures to have survived the nearby battle and raids.

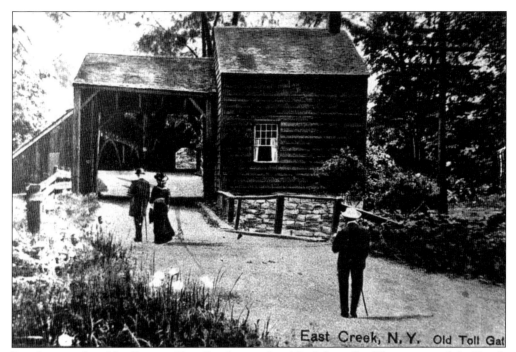

People cross the old tollgate at East Creek, outside of St. Johnsville. The portion of the King's Highway from Schenectady to Utica became known as the Mohawk Turnpike. Tolls were collected to maintain the roads and improve travel. The toll for a horse and rider may have been 5¢, and that for a two-horse wagon may have been 12¢.

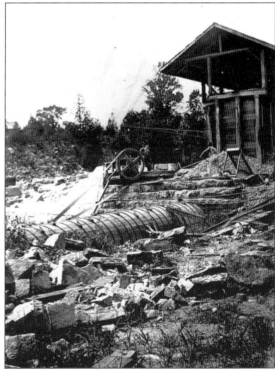

Men work on the East Creek Dam in the early part of the 20th century. Electricity first came to western Montgomery County c. 1890s as a result of one man's vision. Guy Beardslee, by utilizing waterpower from the East Canada Creek, encouraged the novel use of electricity, and in 1898, travelers had a lighted path along Main Street in St. Johnsville. By 1923, demand had prompted the construction of the 90-foot-high dam at East Creek.

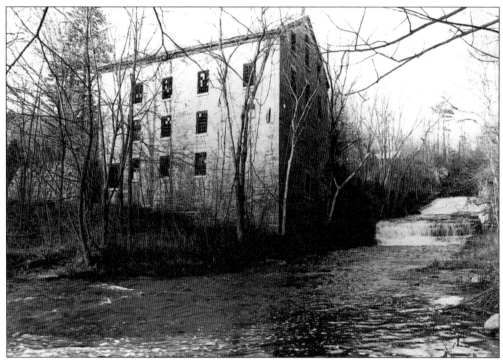

The Leonard & Curran gristmill, located on Klock's Creek, was later owned by Beekman Brothers. Today, visitors can see memorabilia from the Seaman family, even later owners, when staying at the old mill, now renovated into the Inn by the Mill Bed & Breakfast. (Courtesy of Anita Smith, St. Johnsville historian.)

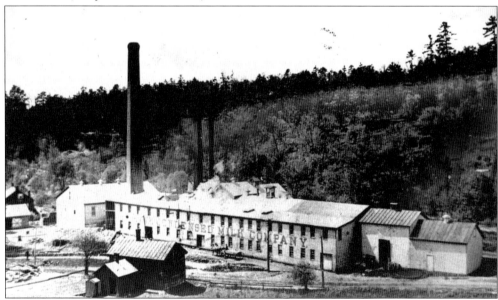

Frank Gebbie and Michael Doyle owned the Mohawk Condensed Milk factory after 1888. Using waterpower from Zimmerman's Creek, local farmers brought their milk to the plant to be processed and condensed for a number of companies. Before 1930, the buildings were converted into the Palatine Dyeing Company. (Courtesy of Anita Smith, St. Johnsville historian.)

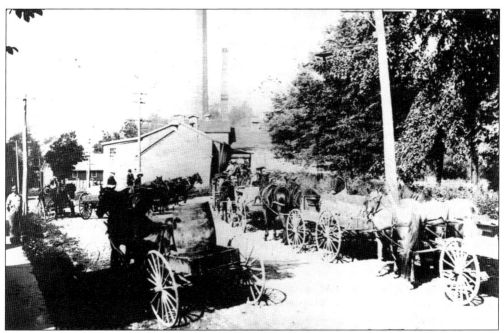

Farmers deliver their excess milk to the Mohawk Condensed Milk factory, on North Division Street. (Courtesy of Anita Smith, St. Johnsville historian.)

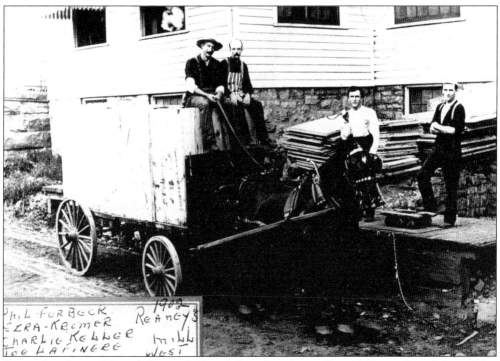

Pictured in front of Joseph Reaney's Royal Gem knitting mill in 1902 are, from left to right, Phil Furbeck, Ezra Kromer, Charlie Keller, Joe LaFinere, and Frank Soules. The mill stood on New Street, in St. Johnsville's west end. (Courtesy of Anita Smith, St. Johnsville historian.)

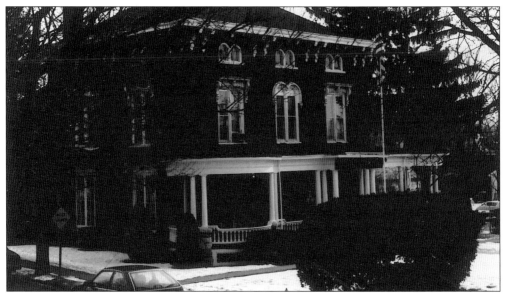

The Bates-Engelhardt Mansion, once the home of industrialist Frederick Engelhardt, was purchased and donated to the village of St. Johnsville in 1933 by Gertrude and Joseph H. Reaney. F. Engelhardt & Sons manufactured player pianos in St. Johnsville from 1889 to the 1930s, when demand fell into decline. The beautiful post–Civil War Italianate mansion, on the corner of Washington and Monroe Streets, now serves as the Community House, home to village municipal offices.

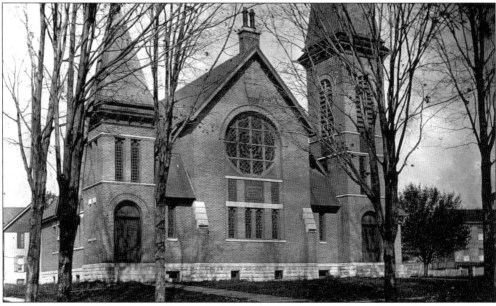

The beginnings of religious worship in St. Johnsville arrived with the Palatine German settlers. The first known church in the Mohawk country was Klock's Church, constructed *c.* 1750 about one mile east of the present village. Incorporated as the Dutch Reformed St. John's Church, the congregation chose to move the church to its present location, erecting a second structure in 1804. Today's church, the congregation's third building, was built on the same site in 1881, this time facing the south.

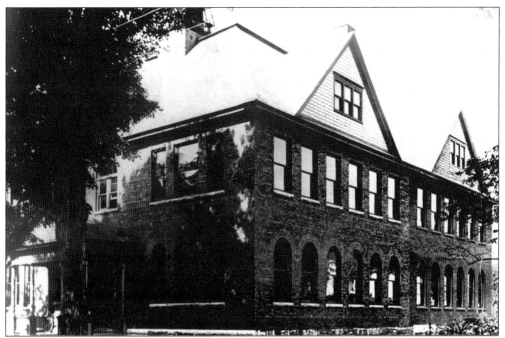

Before construction of the David H. Robbins Elementary School on Monroe Street, students were educated at the St. Johnsville Primary School, on Church Street. Built in the mid-1800s, the wood-frame school building could no longer accommodate the growing student population in the school district. Doors were closed when the present school was opened in January 1952. The building was then razed in the 1970s. (Courtesy of Lois Gruner.)

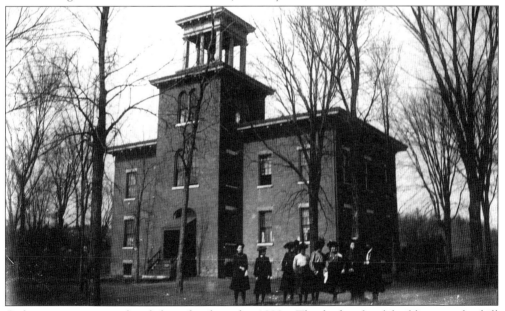

Girls congregate outside of the school in the 1890s. The high school building on the hill was erected c. 1866 on land donated by Absalom Thumb. In 1945, it was destroyed by fire. The present high school was built on the same site. (Courtesy of Anita Smith, St. Johnsville historian.)

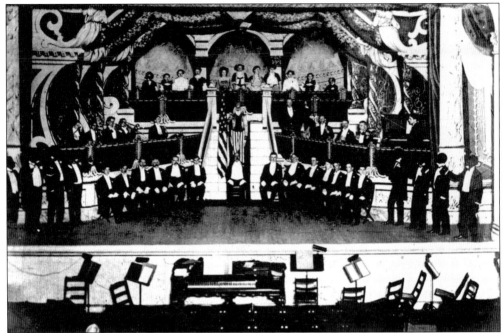

The Whyland Opera House, built on Center Street, was used for plays, vaudeville shows, dances, and concerts. The 1910 minstrel show, seen here, was another type of event held at the four-story structure. Built in 1902, the opera house was ravaged by fire in 1914. (Courtesy of Anita Smith, St. Johnsville historian.)

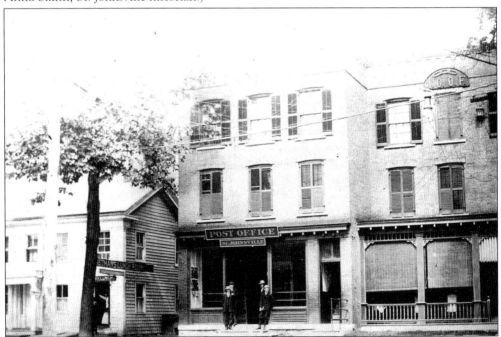

Looking north from Bridge Street, this view shows the old post office in the Mosher Block, now owned by attorney James Conboy. The Getman Lunch Room, to the left, is now the site of the fire station. (Courtesy of Anita Smith, St. Johnsville historian.)

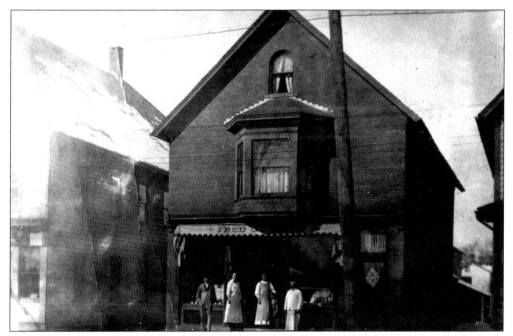

Fred Guhring produced baked goods for St. Johnsville residents at his Bridge Street bakery during the early 1900s. By 1928, Guhring had retired and the bakery was owned by Andrew Barca.

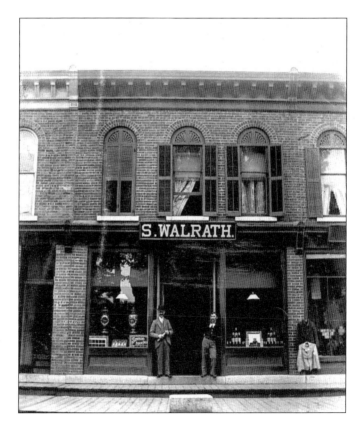

S. Walrath (left) and William Wilsey stand in the doorway of the Walrath drugstore c. 1900. Note the plank sidewalks in front of the store. (Courtesy of Anita Smith, St. Johnsville historian.)

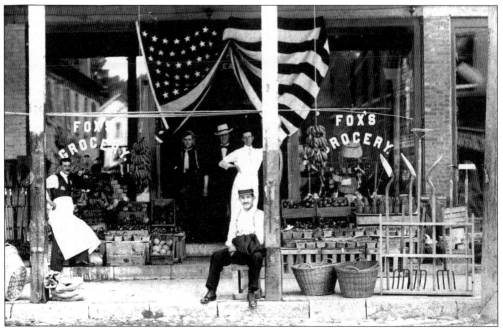

Fox's Grocery was located on West Main Street. Chris Fox stands on the left in this 1912 photograph. (Courtesy of Anita Smith, St. Johnsville historian.)

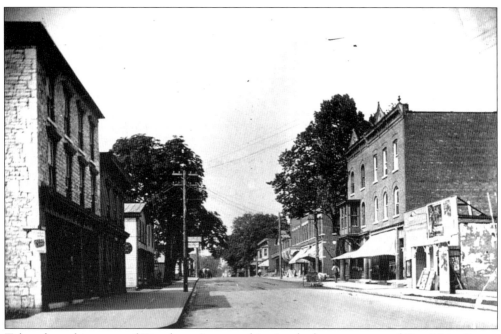

Taken from the corner of Kingsbury Avenue, this view looks at an unpaved East Main Street. Jack Felland's theater is on the right. The Averill Stone Store, on the left, was built in 1830 and demolished in 1982. (Courtesy of Anita Smith, St. Johnsville historian.)